Your Horoscope 2022

....

Aquarius

21 January – 19 February

igloobooks

igloobooks

Published in 2021
First published in the UK by Igloo Books Ltd
An imprint of Igloo Books Ltd
Cottage Farm, NN6 0BJ, UK
Owned by Bonnier Books
Sveavägen 56, Stockholm, Sweden
www.igloobooks.com

0721 001
2 4 6 8 10 9 7 5 3 1
ISBN 978-1-80022-519-0

Written by Belinda Campbell and Denise Evans

Designed by Simon Parker
Edited by Natalie Graham

Printed and manufactured in China

CONTENTS

INTRODUCTION

· · · · · · · · · · · · · · · · ·

This 15-month guide has been designed and written to give a concise and accessible insight into both the nature of your star sign and the year ahead. Divided into two main sections, the first section of this guide will give you an overview of your character in order to help you understand how you think, perceive the world and interact with others and – perhaps just as importantly – why. You'll soon see that your zodiac sign is not just affected by a few stars in the sky, but by planets, elements, and a whole host of other factors, too.

The second section of this guide is made up of daily forecasts. Use these to increase your awareness of what might appear on your horizon so that you're better equipped to deal with the days ahead. While this should never be used to dictate your life, it can be useful to see how your energies might be affected or influenced, which in turn can help you prepare for what life might throw your way.

By the end of these 15 months, these two sections should have given you a deeper understanding and awareness of yourself and, in turn, the world around you. There are never any definite certainties, but with an open mind you will find guidance for what might be, and learn to take more control of your own destiny.

THE CHARACTER OF THE WATER BEARER

. . . .

A rebel in the style of James Dean, with or without a cause, Aquarius is the Water Bearer sign of the zodiac that is here to give to their communities whilst also making waves. With the rebellious songs of the sixties in their ear, breaking tradition and challenging conventions is what this free-thinking air sign is all about. Whilst the songs of the 1960s might lay claim to the age of Aquarius, no one can quite agree on when this sign's astrological age begins or ends. An astrological age is thought to be close to 2000 years long and defined by the associated sign, so why is the age of Aquarius the one that everyone makes a song and dance about? Belonging to the eleventh house in the zodiac calendar that represents community and friendship, Aquarians and their astrological age are sure to influence and change up the whole world and everyone in it as this sign is about realising common goals, hopes and dreams for the future.

Co-ruled by rule-abiding Saturn and rebellious Uranus, Aquarians can be unapologetic when it comes to breaking tradition and will march to the beat of their own drum alone if they must, whether that's to the reggae beat of Bob Marley or the classical compositions of Mozart. Born in the middle of winter, fixed Aquarians may be set in their way of thinking, rightly or wrongly. With a positive energy, Aquarians can be wonderful at acting on what they believe. Aquarian activists Rosa Parks with her Montgomery Bus Boycott and Yoko Ono with her bed-ins for peace show how this sign can act against injustices. Aquarians are known for being progressive thinkers, with an eye fixed firmly on the future, which is perhaps why technological advancements are often closely

linked with this futuristic sign. With Aquarians' devotion to
their social responsibility and the speed at which technology
is sky-rocketing, the age of Aquarius may well be in full
swing as social media activism, or hashtivism, for example in
movements like #TimesUp which continue to gather followers
globally. With influential philanthropists and activists like
Aquarians Ellen DeGeneres and Oprah Winfrey belonging to
this star sign, the voice of Aquarius is sure to be heard for
decades to come.

THE WATER BEARER

Despite being an air sign, it is the giving Water Bearer that
symbolises Aquarius. Ruled by Saturn, who was named after
the Roman god of agriculture, Aquarius' symbol of the Water
Bearer shows the eternal current of positive energy that flows
from this sign and helps the world to grow. The gifts of the
Water Bearer can be numerous, but this air sign is likely to
influence society most substantially through their progressive
thoughts and ideas. Aquarians can be visionaries, and this
air sign's alternative way of thinking combined with their
outgoing nature means that others are likely to listen to what
they have to say. Although not everyone may agree with the
rebel-minded Aquarius, this futuristic thinker is usually ahead
of their time, their symbol of the Water Bearer suggests that
what this sign will bring to the world will be given with the
best of intentions for the goal of a brighter future.

SATURN AND URANUS

The second largest planet in the solar system, Saturn stands out as loud and proud as its co-ruled sign Aquarius. Belonging to the eleventh house of community, this Saturn ruled sign will likely take their social responsibility extremely seriously and may focus all their hard work into building a community that they believe to be just and fair. With the authority of Saturn co-guiding this sign, their fixed way of thinking can at times come across as a little preachy or superior, so this air sign should try to always listen and remain open-minded. Co-ruled by radical Uranus, Aquarians may be all about change and liberation from the rules of Saturn. Uranus is known for its off-kilter axis which could go a long way to explaining the alternative and unconventional traits that some Aquarians can display. Saturn's size and Uranus' unique tilt make these two planets stand out in the solar system and could act as a reminder to all belonging to this extraordinary sign that Aquarians were born to be a little different.

ELEMENTS, MODES AND POLARITIES

Each sign is made up of a unique combination of three defining groups: elements, modes and polarities. Each of these defining parts can manifest themselves in good and bad ways and none should be seen as a positive or a negative – including the polarities! Just like a jigsaw puzzle, piecing these groups together can help illuminate why each sign has certain characteristics and help us find a balance.

ELEMENTS

Fire: Dynamic and adventurous, signs with fire in them can be extroverted. Others are naturally drawn to them because of the positive light they give off, as well as their high levels of energy and confidence.

Earth: Signs with the earth element are steady and driven with their ambitions. They make for a solid friend, parent or partner due to their grounded influence and nurturing nature.

Air: The invisible element that influences each of the other elements significantly, air signs will provide much-needed perspective to others with their fair thinking, verbal skills and key ideas.

Water: Warm in the shallows and freezing as ice. This mysterious element is essential to the growth of everything around it, through its emotional depth and empathy

MODES

Cardinal: Pioneers of the calendar, cardinal signs jump-start each season and are the energetic go-getters.

Fixed: Marking the middle of the calendar, fixed signs firmly denote and value steadiness and reliability.

Mutable: As the seasons end, the mutable signs adapt and give themselves over gladly to the promise of change.

POLARITIES

Positive: Typically extroverted, positive signs take physical action and embrace outside stimulus in their life.

Negative: Usually introverted, negative signs value emotional development and experiencing life from the inside out.

AQUARIUS IN BRIEF

The table below shows the key attributes of Aquarians.
Use it for quick reference and to understand more about this fascinating sign.

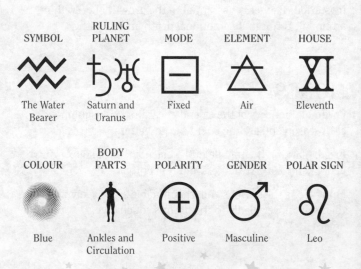

SYMBOL	RULING PLANET	MODE	ELEMENT	HOUSE
The Water Bearer	Saturn and Uranus	Fixed	Air	Eleventh

COLOUR	BODY PARTS	POLARITY	GENDER	POLAR SIGN
Blue	Ankles and Circulation	Positive	Masculine	Leo

ROMANTIC RELATIONSHIPS

. . . .

Aquarians can be some of the friendliest and most alluring of all people and are unlikely to be short of admirers. They may have a laid-back approach to finding a partner, and if they are in a relationship can even seem aloof, but devotion is usually steadfast with this fixed sign. If an Aquarian is not overly emotional with their partner and is much happier to exchange thoughts and ideas than feelings, it is not necessarily because they are not emotionally invested in the relationship. A closed-off Aquarius could struggle with a water sign partner and likewise, water signs might not warm to the cool exterior of this air sign. Warm and passionate fire signs are sure to raise this air sign's temperature and as these elements share a positive outgoing energy, plenty of common interests could be shared. As is the case with many air signs, their love can feel like a trip to the heavens or a painful plummet to Earth. But even if this sign falls out of love, the friendships that they form can be so firm that they can withstand a break-up and be the rule breakers that do in fact stay friends with their exes.

Whilst being highly independent, Aquarians are all about teamwork so can truly thrive in a loving relationship so long as it stems from a firm friendship and mutual beliefs. This giving Water Bearer sign may struggle to give up their prized individualism in exchange for a partnership, and their fixed attitude can give them a stubborn edge that makes them resistant to accepting any dramatic changes to their lifestyle. A partner that understands their Aquarian's desire to remain autonomous and is fully accepting of their uniqueness is one that this sign should try and hold on to. A jealous or possessive lover is a big no-no for this free spirit. Aquarians who want to let love into their lives should understand that change is inevitable and what can feel like an upheaval to their independence is more of a loving revolution.

ARIES: COMPATIBILITY 3/5

Two signs known for their admirable quality of being a good friend to all, Aries and Aquarius should have a good solid foundation of friendship to base their romantic relationship on. This coupling of air and fire will always make for a fuelled love. Independence is key for keeping your Aquarius lover happy, so Aries should be careful with trying to control the relationship or forcing Aquarius to commit too soon. Whilst these two signs have many things in common, it will be discovering each other's differences that will be essential in keeping both partners interested in this relationship.

TAURUS: COMPATIBILITY 1/5

Taurus and Aquarius aren't an obvious match on paper – it's unlikely that these two will find each other on a matchmaking website! The core differences between these signs make a romantic spark unlikely but should not be ruled out. Aquarius is partly ruled by the planet Uranus, symbolising rebellion and change, i.e. some Taureans' worst nightmare. For the easy life-seeking Taurus who likes what they know, the travel-lusting Aquarius can be hard to keep up with. However, these two signs are both fixed and have the potential to make each other stronger if they remain open to change.

GEMINI: COMPATIBILITY 4/5

The individualist sign Aquarius and Twin sign Gemini can make for a compatible trio. Born in the eleventh house that signifies community and friendship, Aquarians thrive in groups and will be a fantastic partner to social butterfly Gemini. The mutable nature of Geminis will mean that they are happy to follow their Aquarian fixed lover's lead which will likely bring a steadiness to the relationship. Being both positive and air signs, these two will have plenty in common. With a Gemini's love for change and an Aquarian's need for progress, these two could create a bright and revolutionary future together.

CANCER: COMPATIBILITY 1/5

The rebellious Aquarius and security seeking Cancer are not always an obvious match romantically. Whilst their core character differences may be the cause of arguments, if these two can find common interests that can cement a foundation for friendship then love could still bloom. If Cancer can help intellectual Aquarius give themselves emotionally to a partner, then both could mutually benefit from this unlikely but special meeting of the heart and mind. Find common ground to share and foreign lands to explore and Aquarius and Cancer could find a lasting love together.

LEO: COMPATIBILITY 5/5

Aquarius is the air sign that sparks the embers of Leo's fire element into full blaze. Opposites on the calendar, this combination of shared positive energy, fixed attitudes and complimentary elements make Leo and Aquarius two individuals that were astrologically made for each other. These unique characters can be guilty of feeling superior to others so may need to remind themselves to treat each other as their rightful equals. Foremost, this is a friendship sprung from fun and crafted by a shared creativity. The visionary mind of Leo combined with Aquarian ideals could have these two creating a utopic life together.

VIRGO: COMPATIBILITY 2/5

Idealist Aquarius and realist Virgo may not be an obvious match, but this couple can be very happy if they find key ideas and goals to share. The organised Virgo will appreciate the Saturn ruled part of Aquarius that represents structure and order but less so their rebellious Uranus side who enjoys throwing the rulebook out. Airy Aquarius and Mercury ruled Virgo are both free thinkers and should be good at allowing each other room to breathe in the relationship which both parties will value in their partner. Optimistic Aquarius and pragmatic Virgo will need to find a shared ambition to balance out their stark differences.

LIBRA: COMPATIBILITY 5/5

When these two air signs of Aquarius and Libra fall in love, it can be a whirlwind romance. Ruled by Venus and Uranus, this may well be a rebellious or radical type of love. Libra is a cardinal sign and is quick to come up with ideas, while an Aquarian's mode is fixed, so makes an ideal partner to actualise their Libra lover's plans. Teamwork really is dreamwork for this outgoing positive couple. The ideals of an Aquarius paired with Libra's righteousness can form a couple that will break down boundaries and create their own rules to make their ideal future.

SCORPIO: COMPATIBILITY 1/5

Mysterious Scorpio and unique Aquarius may well find themselves attracted to one another, but the Scorpion and Water Bearer may need to work hard to keep their relationship off the rocks. Positive Aquarians are outgoing, and socialising in their communities is important. However, this is different for introverted Scorpios, who tend to have a small and intimate circle of friends. Their modes are both fixed, which means they can be resistant to changing their contrasting outlooks. If stable Scorpio can embrace this air sign's free spirited nature and rational Aquarius can provide the intimacy that Scorpio needs, then these two could find their happiness.

SAGITTARIUS: COMPATIBILITY 4/5

Placed two apart on the zodiac calendar, the positive energies of an Aquarian and Sagittarian can be a complimentary and exciting love match. The thrilling ideas of a Sagittarius combined with an Aquarian's independent thinking can mean that these stimulating spouses will have plenty to talk about. The fire in Sagittarius brings an enthusiastic energy to the relationship and the fixed mode of Aquarius can help provide a focus to their ideas and bring them into fruition. Communal minded Aquarius and sociable Sagittarius will likely be at the heart of their shared communities and bring great meaning to each other's lives.

CAPRICORN: COMPATIBILITY 1/5

Both ruled by Saturn, Capricorns and Aquarians will usually have a good understanding of the rules of love. However, Aquarians are co-ruled by Uranus, so may rebel against the traditions that most Capricorns value. A Capricorn and an Aquarius can both be extremely independent people, which may be what attracts them to one another, and as a creative couple they can really bring out the best in each other. This is a union of strong personalities and beliefs that may struggle to find common ground due to their opposite negative and positive energies, although their differences and determination could be their success.

AQUARIUS: COMPATIBILITY 3/5

When two air signs fall in love, it is usually a kindred meeting of the minds, but they should remember to share their hearts too. What may have first started as a friendship, the relationship of two Aquarians is unlikely to be stuck in the mud with both parties interested in progressing their feelings further. As a couple they may challenge the norm and their love can certainly seem radical to outsiders. Both individuals can be guilty of being stubborn or superior so should try loosening up their fixed attitudes. If these two share the same vision their future can be thought provoking and innovative.

PISCES: COMPATIBILITY 2/5

Two very giving signs such as Pisces and Aquarius could happily give themselves to each other in love. Whilst an air and water sign may struggle to understand one another, an Aquarian's intellect combined with a Piscean's compassion can form a relationship that speaks to both the heart and head if flexibility and patience is practised by the pair. A fixed and mutable mode can be a complimentary match, so long as Aquarians don't try to bend the will of their accommodating Piscean partner. The bond that these two can share when at its best can be sincere and spiritually liberating.

FAMILY AND FRIENDS

. . . .

Having a friend in Aquarius is surely having a friend for life. Whether this faithful sign has seen their chums last week or last year, these friendly souls will happily pick up where they last left off. Despite their likeable positive natures, their original and unconventional thoughts can at times make it hard for this sign to relate to their family and friends. Whether the loved ones of an Aquarius believe in the same things as them or not, surrounding themselves with open-minded people who will listen to their vast and sometimes controversial ideas will help this sign form bonds. Befriending a mutable sign like a Piscean or Sagittarian who will usually welcome a change of perspective could help Aquarians air their ideas freely and without judgment. For an intellectual chat or non-stop gossip, air signs like Libra and Gemini will always be happy to exchange ideas and chat endlessly with their Aquarian friend. Born in the eleventh house of friendship and community, being a member of a club or society is where Aquarians can feel most at home. There can be a secret side to Aquarius, some will certainly value their privacy, so perhaps a secret society or hanging out in a bar off the beaten track will be where to find this sign catching up with friends.

Aquarius' uniqueness could extend to their choice of home as this sign may find that they do not feel comfortable in a traditional setting such as a two-up two-down terraced house. Instead, they may feel more at home in a converted barn or church, or whatever perhaps best suits their one-off personality. Inside an Aquarian's home, their choice of interior is likely to continue to reflect their utterly unique personality; think eclectic and antique trinkets rather than Swedish flat-pack furniture. Wherever this nomadic character decides to settle, building a social network will be key to them and they will no doubt be a positive pillar in their community. Symbolised by the Water Bearer, Aquarians are intent on making their community flourish and their giving and friendly ways will usually have them working in a team for the greater good. This Water Bearer might be found raising money for their local watering hole or at the local council meeting speaking their mind on how to best improve their local area for the benefit of everyone.

When it comes to the family of an Aquarian, they will always try to work as a team. Born in the eleventh house where teamwork is key, Aquarians may be the one that encourages each member of the family to vocalise their thoughts and have a vital input into the way they function as a household. As with their own life, Aquarians may favour an alternative path for their children also. Home schooling may be an Aquarian's preference if they find that their local schools are too traditional for their liking. Aquarians will not want their children to miss out on group activities so enrolling their child in sports or other social clubs could be a priority. However, as with any functional community, the voice of everyone will be heard in an Aquarian's home and their children may have the deciding vote or at least a valid input.

MONEY AND
CAREERS

. . . .

Being a certain star sign will not dictate the type of career
that you have, although the characteristics that fall under
each sign could help you identify the areas in which you could
potentially thrive. Conversely, to succeed in the workplace, it is
just as important to understand what you are good at as it is to
know what you are less brilliant at so that you can see the areas
in which you will need to perhaps work harder to achieve your
career and financial goals.

When it comes to money, Aquarians are usually far more
interested in the exchange of ideas than of cash. If an Aquarian
is money focused it will generally be because they want to help
their community in some way. To their friends and family,
Aquarius is known for their seemingly endless generosity and
this Water Bearer will come to parties with their arms full of
wine and treats for all. This sign is normally fixated on doing
things for the benefit of their fellow human so raising funds
for a local charity or donating their money to help restore a
nearby youth hostel are the types of projects that this giving
sign may like to spend their money on. Aquarians won't
typically be satisfied with donating just their money to the
good of the community and may find that their vocation is
working as a social worker or in another public sector where
they believe they can best serve their community and make
a difference, like human rights lawyer Amal Clooney, equal
rights campaigner Rosa Parks or suffragette Susan B. Anthony.
Aquarians want to make their communities better places and
make a difference for everyone.

As an air sign, a career that stretches their mind should be
well suited to an Aquarian. This futuristic sign could be set

on inventing the next world-changing invention, theory, or technological advancement like Aquarians Thomas Edison or Charles Darwin. So innovative and outspoken is this sign that people are certainly inclined to listen to them in the workplace, even if their colleagues don't quite agree with their unique perspective. With Saturn by their side, Aquarians will usually be highly devoted to their work responsibilities and can be one of the most reliable and hard-working of signs. The authority given to this sign by Saturn could help Aquarians become a highly successful team manager or commanding boss of their own company, like Duncan Bannatyne. Their positive energy can be a stimulating force in the office, and being born in the eleventh house makes them both inspiring leaders and energetic team players – look at famous Aquarians Abraham Lincoln or Franklin D. Roosevelt to see how this sign can take charge and inspire people even in the trickiest of situations.

Whilst you can't always choose who you work with, it can be advantageous to learn about colleagues' key characteristics through their star signs to try and work out the best ways of working with them. Feeling the influence of radical Uranus can make it hard for Aquarians to follow someone else's rules, so their relationships with managers and bosses could be challenging at times if they do not share the same ethos. Born in the first house that represents the self, Aries could be a colleague that jars with the community-minded Aquarius, whilst fellow air sign Libra could be the pioneering idea-seeking boss that gels well with Aquarius.

HEALTH AND WELLBEING

. . . .

Another way in which this air sign can help clear their mind is by making sure that their environment is both peaceful and functional. Ensuring that their element of air can flow freely throughout their household may be an Aquarian's priority, so introducing the Chinese practice of feng shui into their home and office space could help restore some harmony.

Associated with blood circulation, an adrenaline fuelled sport that gets an Aquarian's blood pumping could be how this energetic sign likes to stay fit and healthy. This alternative air sign might literally be in their element taking on daring sports like base jumping or paragliding. Or if heights aren't an Aquarian's thing, skiing or snowboarding off piste somewhere a little different in the world might be more suited to this unconventional sign. After an active day on the slopes, a little *après ski* sauna will no doubt be where Aquarians make a beeline for in order to give their tired muscles and blood circulation that extra boost.

Having a healthy cholesterol level is essential for everyone wanting to live a long and healthy life, but it may be something that this sign is more keenly aware of to keep their associated body system of blood circulation thriving. Eating healthily is a great way to feel healthier and a proven way to naturally lower a high cholesterol, so if this is a concern for any star sign, reducing their intake of foods that are high in saturated fats such as red meat and cheese is always a good place to start. Making a few adjustments to diet, such as ordering the tuna steak rather than the beef, should boost the body with healthier omega three fats and have any sign, Aquarius included, feeling much healthier. Aquarians should try not being a total stranger to their local GP, even if they prefer to practise alternative home remedies to battle the flu rather than get their annual jab, and always seek professional guidance if they have concerns about their health.

Mental health should be tended to just as readily as physical health and, as for any air sign, having a happy and clear mind is essential to an Aquarian's wellbeing. If an Aquarian's head is feeling clogged up with stress or worries, their usually innovative and free-flowing ideas can feel blocked, which can compound an air sign's anxiety. Identifying the root of the problem could be the first step as the cause of anxiety may or may not be obvious. By tackling issues candidly, an Aquarian can then plan the most practical route to a happy solution, which could include turning to their beloved community, be it a neighbour or sibling, and asking for help.

Aquarius

....

DAILY FORECASTS
for 2021

OCTOBER

. . . .

Friday 1st

Partner time can help to chase the blues away. You may be stubborn and resist any inner work presented to you because today is all about how you are seen. You desire to get out and be loud and visible. Let yourself go for one night only.

Saturday 2nd

Family duties may have to be put on hold today and this may cause friction. You may not realise it, but things are shifting naturally now. Your career is highlighted and gives you more joy. This may be what was needed to change. Free up more time for fun in the future.

Sunday 3rd

A quiet Sunday is needed in order to prepare for the coming week. You may have to get deep into your accounts or do some cleaning. Mercury may give you big problems today which can affect your happy mood. If you feel stuck, take a break and return with fresh eyes.

Monday 4th

Try to refrain from making an impulse buy today. Get serious and not frivolous. Your bank balance may not support a major purchase right now. If you're pining after something you desire, make a list of the pros and cons involved and give yourself a reality check.

Tuesday 5th

You may be more grounded today and accept that hard work is necessary before you reap any rewards. You have the ability to get to the bottom of something deep and your detective-like vigilance will be noted by those above you. Persuasion is your greatest ally so use it.

Wednesday 6th

A new moon occurs in your travel sector. This Moon meets Mars and makes you driven to set goals and intentions regarding long-distance travel and higher education. Pluto turns direct and you may feel the shift as a lightening of your load. Constantly reinventing yourself is exhausting you.

Thursday 7th

It's possible that you feel some tension as the Moon squares off with newly direct Pluto. You may feel an emotional pull towards all that you have let go of this year, including part of your old identity. Venus glides into your social sector. Watch the invitations flood in now.

Friday 8th

The Sun and Mars are having a prolonged meet in your travel sector. This powerhouse of energy is ripe for you to commence your new moon intentions. You may need to be strict with yourself and upset some family members but stick to your guns, the only way is up.

Saturday 9th

Today's energy can weigh heavy on you. Mercury joins the Sun and Mars and you may experience confusion, doubt and a relapse of your resolve. This will pass, so distract yourself with quality time with your friends. Online associates can also help alleviate the stress you feel today.

Sunday 10th

Your ruler, Saturn, turns direct today. Your mood changes and you're more uplifted and hopeful. You seem to have broken through the brain-fog caused by Mercury and have your ego and drive back on track. Put your best foot forward now and implement your intentions.

Monday 11th

The week begins with the Moon still hanging about in your social sector, maybe you didn't have time to connect with everyone at the weekend and are still catching up. A person you admire gets your attention and time is well spent listening to their tales. Winding down this evening should be easy.

Tuesday 12th

Today you may stir something up in your family sector. This will ultimately be beneficial to your inner work. Something from the past may come up to be reviewed and healed. There may even be an unexpected surprise connected with a revelation. You may do a regular chore in a different way.

Wednesday 13th

The Moon meets newly direct Pluto. Take some time to listen to your inner voice and the praise it is giving you. Change is always difficult, but you have mastered that while Pluto has been in your hidden sector. You are permitted to see how your dreams might manifest.

Thursday 14th

In your sign, the Moon meets Saturn. Your wise but harsh teacher rewards you for the inner work you've done this year. Responsibilities don't have to be dull. Selfishness is not pretty. Personal boundaries are paramount. Well done for learning something new and accepting it as truth.

Friday 15th

Jupiter is giving you one last lesson before he too turns direct. What have you learned about truth, law, joy, and broadening your horizons whilst he has been in your sign? Take one last look around and ensure that your unique personality has uplifted those around you and benefited all.

Saturday 16th

You may enjoy a dreamy day today and follow your heart. There may be reminders of past losses and achievements, but you will also see future plans and how to develop them. Take a day of doing nothing except merging with things and people that you value highly.

Sunday 17th

Jupiter is now direct and will continue his journey through your sign. You may now step up your game and bounce happily through life knowing you are supported. When the Moon meets Neptune, you feel totally aligned with your true north and appreciate the process you have gone through this year.

Monday 18th

Mercury also turns direct now. You may make travel arrangements and review contracts or commitments you may have put on hold. Your communications sector will be buzzing with life. Write everything down in your planner and get ready to be the life and soul of upcoming parties.

Tuesday 19th

The Moon and Mercury are opposing each other, and you have a lot of information to sift through. Prioritise these and give yourself time to plan thoroughly. Mars and Jupiter combine to help you make long-distance travel a real possibility. Other cultures call you, as does higher education. Your social life is taking off.

Wednesday 20th

You may feel the strain of recent activity today. Mars energy is being drained by the opposing full moon in your communications sector. It's likely that a project has come to fruition and needs your full attention. There may be something to celebrate today. Go easy on yourself.

Thursday 21st

The Moon is now in your family sector and meets Uranus. This can be a volatile time as usual and you may need extra help around the house. Don't try doing it all alone as there's a chance of burn-out. Ask others to help you do the mundane chores.

Friday 22nd

Mars is squaring off with Pluto which may cause you to hide and isolate yourself. Think of it as self-preservation. You have to submit to time off if you need to keep energy for the things you enjoy most. Earthy grounded activities will help you stay focused and on task.

Saturday 23rd

The Sun enters your career sector and will aid in problem-solving. It will also highlight some nastiness or gossip in and around the workplace. You may experience jealousy as people may resent your climb to the top of the corporate ladder. Express yourself carefully with certain people.

Sunday 24th

There's a high chance that you speak out of turn today and upset someone from your social circle. Discord worries you and you should aim to put this right at the earliest opportunity. It may not be as serious as you think. You've simply said the wrong thing to the wrong person.

Monday 25th

You have an urge to take some steps towards your true north. Your path in life is right before your eyes and you must step forward bravely. Jupiter and Mars can help you to be courageous and remain optimistic about this. Don't let Neptune fool you.

Tuesday 26th

Your social circle may be casting doubts about your new ventures. This may be someone who's jealous of your trust in the universe and wishes they had the same opportunity. Be kind and compassionate to them. Tell them your story and they may begin to write their own.

Wednesday 27th

You may be exhausted by your mundane duties. Self-care is important. Neptune is still causing confusion and you may feel some doubt. Nurture yourself back to good mental health and you'll see that this was just a passing phase that you felt because you were in the flow.

Thursday 28th

If you feel drained, ask a partner to lift you up and take the lead. You'll feed off the attentive and vibrant personality and this will be enough to restore your normal easy-going nature. There's a party animal inside you just waiting to get out.

Friday 29th

Family and partners may both be requiring your presence today. This might be difficult to manage, and you'll need to do what's best for you, not them. Mercury lends you the gift of the gab and you can persuade others to do your bidding. People will fall in line once they know your feelings.

Saturday 30th

Mars enters your career sector with great force. With his help, you can storm through your daily work and complete project after project. This can also be a decluttering process where you review your work duties and ascertain whether they're really worth your effort.

Sunday 31st

Today you think and feel everything deeply. You may have a lot to express but have the good sense to process it all first. Uranus is bubbling inside your family sector and you may find a solution to a problem come up from nowhere. Your ego and emotions are in sync.

NOVEMBER
....

Monday 1st

You achieve more balance and look to outside activities to keep you afloat. Stretching your wings is natural for an air sign but grounding yourself is a problem. Educational studies can do this for you right now. Look for a new avenue to explore. This could become part of your current transformation.

Tuesday 2nd

Today you struggle as you fail to see that allowing yourself some down time is the best thing for you at the moment. Saturn supports you and asks you to see that your personal boundaries need strengthening. You don't have to be everything for everybody.

Wednesday 3rd

The Moon meets Mercury and you may find that you're going over and over certain thoughts and getting nowhere. Discuss this with someone you trust. You may experience some confusion as your road ahead looks very different from how you first imagined it. Trust that you will always be guided towards your best self.

Thursday 4th

The Moon meets Mars before becoming new in your career sector. This is time to review your social status and ask yourself if it's working for you. Transform or discard things that are weighing you down. You may find that you do this impulsively or very suddenly today.

Friday 5th

Venus has entered your hidden sector and will help you to love alone time more. Any inner work done while she's here will be tempered with compassion for yourself. Mercury moves into your high-flying career sector and will up the ante in your communication skills in the workplace.

Saturday 6th

The Moon shifts just in time for the weekend. A social event with your wider groups may be the perfect excuse to let off steam and party the night away. This may possibly be with work colleagues. Mercury talks to Venus about making subtle shifts at work. This might help alleviate some stress.

Sunday 7th

You have no time for dreaming today unless it's with friends who share your vision. You may be more inclined towards those who are outgoing and driven than those who are spiritual and ethereal. Plans for the upcoming festivities can excite you. You may have a leading role to play here.

Monday 8th

Today can have a seductive quality that you lap up and enjoy. The Moon meets Venus in your hidden sector and connects to Mars and the Sun. Passion and romance are favoured and there may be a secret rendezvous on the agenda. Something new gives you goosebumps.

Tuesday 9th

Pluto hosts the Moon for her monthly visit. You may find that you're emotionally attached to re-inventing yourself again. Now that you've come to terms with it, it sounds like the best thing you can do. Be patient as this may take some time.

Wednesday 10th

Heavy energy may drain you today. Although the Moon is in your sign, it connects poorly to other planets and you may feel restricted, fatigued and exposed. Mercury and Mars in your career sector may be responsible for high activity and a list of deadlines you need to meet before the week is out.

Thursday 11th

Your nerves may be frazzled and there's a possibility that you take it out on your nearest and dearest. Jupiter makes things larger and you may find that squabbles get out of control very quickly. Rein them in by being fluid and adaptable to any change that comes.

Friday 12th

A little help from Venus goes a long way today. You're mindful of the need to withdraw into yourself if things get too much. This would be a good time to pause and reflect on the year gone by. You may rediscover skills and talents that you can use again.

Saturday 13th

Be very careful what you say, as you may inadvertently slip up and betray a confidence. Your mind is not on your job and you're at risk of drifting off. Your true north has gripped you and won't let go. Hang in there and enjoy the moment.

Sunday 14th

Water energy makes you more sensitive to others' needs. A new romance may be blossoming or is hidden behind a veil from the outside world. Is this a secret or are you being protective? How does this fit in with the new you? Is it part of your progress?

Monday 15th

You may be fired up with a list of chores to do. This might have an impact on your inner strength, and you may feel resentful that you have no time for yourself. Do your duty but no more, you'll have to be strong and say no.

Tuesday 16th

Today may be very busy as your communications sector is highlighted. There may be many messages to make or plans to negotiate. If you're doing something for a wider group, ensure that all the work doesn't fall on your shoulders. Share the love and share the workload.

Wednesday 17th

Volatile energy makes today very tricky for you. You may be caught in the crossfire of work and home problems. Nothing seems very easy at the moment and you are not enjoying home life as you should. You just want to get away from it all somehow.

Thursday 18th

The rollercoaster of managing work and home duties may come to a head today. Someone, maybe you, will have a tantrum and the tension will be broken. Know that this opens up lines of communication to resolve this problem. Mercury may win you round with promising words and dreams.

Friday 19th

There's a full moon in your family sector which will throw a spotlight on the recent tension and you may see that this has been coming for a long time. Venus talks nicely to Uranus and people may begin to see how negatively you've been affected by taking on all the work.

Saturday 20th

Take a day and use your creative talents to describe your emotions. You may not be able to get a grip on them any other way. Listening to music will be a great therapeutic exercise. Someone may try to bully you today, but they won't get far.

Sunday 21st

Artistic endeavours may feel blocked as the Moon squares off with dreamy Neptune. You have an urge to switch off from outside life and do your own thing. Pay a visit to someone you trust and have a heart to heart. This may be good for your self-esteem.

Monday 22nd

Today is far more nurturing. You recognise the need to do your everyday duties and leave time for yourself. A secret meeting or time spent with maternal figures will nourish your senses and make you feel good. Happiness is not hard to find now so grab it with both hands.

Tuesday 23rd

You may be enjoying time with a person who cares for you so much that you seem to forget how to care for yourself. Venus gives you a nudge and asks you to be on your guard. You may be excitable, unpredictable and too dreamy for your own good today.

Wednesday 24th

A sudden urge to break free tells you that you've had enough of being smothered with love for now. It may even feel controlling and this makes you revolt. You desire partner time where you feel you can show off and parade with someone who has more confidence than you.

Thursday 25th

Mars and Venus are making a helpful connection for would-be lovers. Perhaps this is done behind closed doors. Be careful as there may be some passive-aggressive behaviour going on and this coupling may, in fact, be rather toxic for you. Stand up and be seen. Be loud and proud.

Friday 26th

A fiery Moon in your relationship sector opposes Jupiter. What has the lucky planet seen and not agreed with? You may find that you've come to a sticking point, even if just momentarily. Do your partner's needs and visions meet your own? Review this question now.

Saturday 27th

Your heart and head are not in sync. There's no point trying to reconcile them as they won't agree. You may think that you're being flexible, but you're actually being non-committal. Give up trying for today and come back to it when the Moon shifts.

Sunday 28th

Today, you need answers. You've been through your inner filing cabinet and found gaps. You may be prepared to go the extra mile for a person you care about, but they're not being totally honest with you. Root out the cause of this and discuss things openly.

Monday 29th

Mercury is in the heart of the Sun and saying nothing. Your social sector may seem busy and superficial. It's your job to listen for subtle messages and look out for signposts. These may tell you something about how your wider groups are operating. Why have you missed this until now?

Tuesday 30th

The energy today suggests that you compare your agenda to those of people around you. They may seem to match but do they really? How might you ensure that personal boundaries aren't breached, and that each person has total respect from others? Make agreements or contracts within your groups.

DECEMBER

······················

Wednesday 1st

The big news is that Neptune has turned direct. You may now get more in line with your inner compass. Remember that he resides in your money sector and you will need to hold on to your cash and not let it slip away. You can determine fantasies from real dreams now.

Thursday 2nd

The Moon opposes Uranus and you may see the familiar conflicts between your home and work lives. Responsibilities regarding both may be difficult to manage under this influence. You're more inclined to see to yourself first and others second. Be sure not to let people down today.

Friday 3rd

The Moon meets fiery Mars in your career sector. You may be rushing or extra motivated to finish up jobs and meet deadlines. This may put extra pressure on your duties to yourself and wider groups but will need to be done. Stay strong as this won't last long.

Saturday 4th

A new moon in your social sector is a great chance to make plans that are big, bold and adventurous. Speak to your interest groups and get advice or ideas to stretch yourself in the next six months. Maybe a visit to a long-distance friend will suffice. Keep it real and do-able.

Sunday 5th

Make the most of Jupiter's energy in your sign before he leaves. Broaden your outlook and think about how different cultures and overseas trips might advance your knowledge and understanding of yourself. Take some time this evening to process your thoughts and make a game plan for the coming year.

Monday 6th

Today has great energy for you to access and use in all walks of life. You may be quietly planning surprises for the family whilst idly dreaming about your bigger vision. Mars and Pluto talk and help you to take action where appropriate and make changes that will be worthwhile.

Tuesday 7th

The Moon meets Pluto in your hidden sector. You may feel more positive this month and no longer feel that you're being threatened with too much change and adjustment. This afternoon the Moon drops into your sign and you can put your best foot forward and show up to life.

Wednesday 8th

You may need to pull back a little today and remember where your duties are. It's possible that you're trying to run before you can walk. Agitations from your home will likely be the reason for this. You desire to get going but there's a red light stopping you.

Thursday 9th

The Moon and Jupiter meet in your sign. You may find that
any tension will feel bigger than it needs to be. Stop, pause and
breathe before you do anything. Take in the wider picture before
acting. Find that altruistic side of you and put others first.

Friday 10th

You may well be spending too much money today, but it will
be well spent. The Moon is in your money sector connecting
to Uranus in your home sector. This could be your festive
shopping day. Uranus likes surprises and so do you. You
especially like giving them to others.

Saturday 11th

Venus meets Pluto today in your hidden sector. This is important
as she will retrograde soon. Love, harmony and beauty must be
combined with change and transformation. Perhaps you've had a
change of heart about someone who you believe has wronged you.
Perhaps you're considering a whole new you.

Sunday 12th

Today will be filled with communication of all sorts. There
may be many plans to be made for the festive season so get out
your planner and make sure you enter everything. You're very
happy when filling up your time. Check your bank balance
allows for this much activity.

Monday 13th

Mercury enters your hidden sector while Mars marches into
your social sector. This heralds a time of hedonistic fun with
friends and then reprimanding yourself when alone. You could
overdo the good things in life now and fret about it later.
Exercise some self-discipline.

Tuesday 14th

You may have trouble pleasing yourself as others demand too much of your attention. There's a possibility that you exhaust yourself for the sake of the family. Self-talk can be positive if you run your thoughts through the good reasons you have for doing this but remember to take care of your own needs too.

Wednesday 15th

The tension that comes with this season catches up with you. There may be conflict in the family. You can be stubborn and unmoving or quite the opposite and go too far with someone. Expect a blow-out of some sort as tempers may be frayed.

Thursday 16th

Today there's better energy which can help to soothe family squabbles. Your innermost thoughts are already transforming themselves to help you deal with the delicate balance of yours and others' needs. You may feel like hosting an early party tonight. Once again, you will need to curb your spending.

Friday 17th

The Moon sits opposite Mars and this energy can make you drained. Your emotional needs are to create, make love or music but your wider groups are calling for your presence. In this case, the groups will win as it's easier for you to let off steam with them.

Saturday 18th

You still have the creative buzz running within you and you may have time to do something about it today. A vision board for next year containing all the new plans and dreams you have will be a good exercise. You're adaptable and moody so use those feelings to create.

Sunday 19th

Venus turns retrograde. Over the next forty days, you may see an old lover return or your current one disappear. In your hidden sector, you may also see profound change from deep inside you. A full moon lights up your creative sector and puts your talents in the spotlight.

Monday 20th

This may be a lucky day with surprises coming your way. You may have the need to be nurtured and looked after but also a conflicting need to break free from confines. Feminine wisdom will come to you today and you need to listen. Something will trigger an old wound.

Tuesday 21st

The winter solstice takes place as the Sun enters your hidden sector. You may find this month uncomfortable as your innermost thoughts and processes may be revealed. Take this time to pause and reflect on the year gone by. Reward yourself for the hard work you have done.

Wednesday 22nd

Partner time may help you to come out of a quiet zone and give you freedom of speech. Choose someone you trust and relate to well. You may need to get things off your chest in a safe place. Be bold and brave as your relationship sector is highlighted.

Thursday 23rd

Today is another chance to pause. The Moon is safely in your relationship sector and you may enjoy time with a lover which is uninterrupted by outside influences. Jupiter is about to leave your sign; how can you thank the lucky planet for his stay? Can you do something brave?

Friday 24th

You may feel over-emotional and pull back from relating to others. You might feel the need to have a clear out or isolate yourself. Tension could arise in your family and social sectors. There are too many people demanding your attention and you desire to run and hide.

Saturday 25th

Try to stay grounded and be as practical as possible today. The planetary energy supports this as the best way to get through the day. Issues surrounding self-care or ex-lovers may surface as Venus has retrograded back to meet Pluto. You may experience some subtle manipulation today.

Sunday 26th

The Moon connects to Venus and Pluto making you emotionally invested in whatever Venus retrograde has brought up for you. You deal with it responsibly and can decide to put it to one side for now. Your thought processes surrounding this are logical and you may begin to see another point of view.

Monday 27th

Today you can achieve more balance, but you may use distractions such as your friendship groups. Are you avoiding dealing with a nasty situation? Putting up a personal boundary and sticking to it may be a better way of handling this. Use your Mars energy to defend you.

Tuesday 28th

You may be feeling burnt out by recent activity and the best thing you can do is hide away with a good book. Your thoughts are doing overtime, your self-care is poor, and you feel victimised or manipulated. Say goodbye to Jupiter as he leaves your sign.

Wednesday 29th

Jupiter now enters your money and value house. This is a lucky sign if you're wishing to improve your financial situation. It's also beneficial as you'll start to see your own self-worth in a different way. You may be too hard on yourself today and this will need to change.

Thursday 30th

As the year draws to a close you may find that your thoughts are filled with your dreams for the future and your inner transformation. Mercury meets Pluto and they discuss your progress so far. The next stage of your development is about to begin.

Friday 31st

The Moon meets up with Mars in your social sector which is just the energy you need for a great festive celebration with friends. You may look back on the year gone by and vow to honour the heavy demands of your ruler Saturn as he strives to make you a better person.

Aquarius

· · · · · · · · · · · · · ·

DAILY FORECASTS
for 2022

JANUARY

....

Saturday 1st

Happy New Year and welcome to 2022. You may choose to begin the year in quiet contemplation. This may also be more of a recovery time after a busy couple of weeks. You feel the need to come back to yourself and take a look at what really matters to you.

Sunday 2nd

A lot of shifting and rearranging of old thoughts and habits may have unsettled you. A new moon in your most private area of life helps you to make those new year resolutions about balancing work and private time. Networking will be a theme for the next few weeks. Get out there and show yourself off.

Monday 3rd

An old love may have haunted you recently. This may come to a head today and you will need to deal with it once more. This will not be the last time it appears, and you may feel unsure or tempted to have them in your life again. Think twice today.

Tuesday 4th

Your head and heart may appear as if they are in sync, but are you sure you are not convincing yourself that something is right when it isn't? Don't be allured by ideals and romanticism. Your ruler, Saturn, urges caution and asks that you protect your boundaries.

Wednesday 5th

Ask your closest friends and social groups for advice today.
This may involve going further afield than you usually do.
Broaden your mind and listen to what they have to offer. It
may be that you need help to proceed with a plan that you find
unusual, eccentric or too complicated.

Thursday 6th

Realise the need for a final push on a project. This could be
a completion or abandonment and may leave you conflicted.
However, you have a big heart and have no difficulty expressing
that today. This will help get things shifted in one direction or
another. Home life may bring surprises.

Friday 7th

A little of what you fancy does you good today. You might hit
the sales and find something which is a little frivolous but
brings you joy. Self-care can include treating yourself. You may
now be thinking about how to align your plans with your true
self and live your best life.

Saturday 8th

Your energy lifts and today may see you making many visits or
calls to put plans in action. Take in all the details and absorb
what you feel comfortable with. Research will be fruitful now
as your mind is geared up to make positive change in your life.

Sunday 9th

You may have a setback today and realise that unfinished
business still lingers. This may play on your mind and make
you restless and anxious. If you remember to keep your
boundaries healthy and your energy focused on the new, you
will be able to manage this tricky episode with compassion.

Monday 10th

Being out and about today can make you tired and irritable. You may feel as if you have got nothing done. Returning to your own home may bring more pleasure as you can relax in your own surroundings and dance to your own tune. Make a nice plan for this evening.

Tuesday 11th

Today you get a glimpse of your true north. Where would you like to be heading in your life? You must be careful with whom you network or connect as things may not go your way. Be open to seeing another point of view or risk having a tantrum.

Wednesday 12th

If you need to make changes or permanent endings, then today has the right energy for you to achieve this. You may notice who is on your team and who needs to be left on the sidelines. Those you define as family are ready to support you.

Thursday 13th

Mercury begins his first retrograde tomorrow and you may feel some effects today. Back up all your devices, double check travel plans and ensure that your communication is clear and precise. Any research and developments you have made can be put on hold and given a thorough review at this time.

Friday 14th

If you feel as if the year has already gone weird, don't worry. This is your chance to make sure that what you had already taken on board is right for you. It may be that you have taken on too much and now need to slim it down to what is achievable.

Saturday 15th

Take some time today to ensure that your basic needs are
being met. You may feel that you are giving more than you are
getting. Buy nourishing foods, watch your favourite movies
and give yourself a day of home comforts. Make yourself feel
safe and protected.

Sunday 16th

A startling realisation may come to you this afternoon. This
may be an old wound you thought had healed. Sharp words
from family members may shock you. Retreat under the
blanket and process this. An old lover may trigger feelings you
would rather not have to deal with.

Monday 17th

A full moon shines its light on how well you take care of
yourself. You may feel slightly manipulated or controlled by
another. Keep on going with the self-care routine just a little
longer until you are nurtured, nourished and strong enough to
come out of your hole and face the world.

Tuesday 18th

Today you may notice how much a partner means to you. They
may have been the one who has coaxed you back into the world
and lifted your spirits. You will certainly be in the mood for
a bit of love and romance. Make sure that you communicate
your feelings clearly.

Wednesday 19th

You may have some trouble with authority figures today. This is because you have your own way of doing things and are unwilling to try another. You may have a mini tantrum until you see that there is no work-around and you simply must do what you are being told.

Thursday 20th

The Sun enters your sign today, happy birthday. You have the energy to get things going and this may involve a friendship group or another social circle. Check all the details if this is a deeply intense time and don't get caught out by misunderstandings within your groups.

Friday 21st

You may be tempted to sacrifice or surrender to something which brought you pleasure in the past. This could also be old coping mechanisms and addictions. If you stay aware, you may find an innovative way of solving an old problem which has resurfaced and is causing you stress and tension.

Saturday 22nd

Today you will be consumed by doing jobs and chores for other people. You may not get enough time to do your own jobs. However, this is done with good faith and you manage to shed a load which has been bothering you. You end the day feeling more balanced.

Sunday 23rd

Mercury is in the heart of the Sun and your mind may be fuzzy. If you find it difficult to articulate, then be the listener. You may receive more wisdom today by being aware of your inner voice, symbols and dreams. A last-minute invitation from friends may come your way.

Monday 24th

The next few weeks may find you more driven to explore your inner workings. You may be relentlessly diving for pearls of wisdom or golden nuggets. The thing you have to master is to recognise what is worthy of all this effort. Some things need healing, some need laying to rest.

Tuesday 25th

There is a lot of activity for your emotional self to deal with today. You may prefer to concentrate on your own issues, but family matters also need your attention. Your work and career are most at risk as you are being distracted by other things today.

Wednesday 26th

Self-enquiry heats up now. It may feel like something is coming at you from two sides and you need to duck or talk your way out of a situation. There is a possibility that you have become involved in a situation from the past which is re-playing either in your head or in real life.

Thursday 27th

If you are serious about letting go of something and leaving it well and truly in the past, then today has the right energy for you. You may not feel good about it and it could reopen old wounds. Check-in with your friends and support groups.

Friday 28th

You may have dodged a bullet. If you have strong and healthy boundaries, you may have deflected more damage than you think. Give yourself a clap for being defensive yet responsible. Another perspective comes in handy now, but you may not see this at first.

Saturday 29th

Listen carefully to your inner voice as you may find a new direction or a loophole in an old plan. Something needs to be re-written in your mind before implementing new ideas. Today is filled with emotional awareness and revelations. Let something go with love and give gratitude for the lessons it brought.

Sunday 30th

You may be craving a little self-care, a treat or a loving touch today. Do what you can to fill that need. You may have to let someone down this evening as you concentrate on filling your own cup first. This may cause some tension so be kind and respectful.

Monday 31st

A sleepless night may leave you feeling irritable today. Triggers may have returned in the darkness to make you doubt and question your deepest feelings. Note them and deal with them after you have ruminated for some time. Step into the week ready to face whatever is aimed at you.

FEBRUARY

....

Tuesday 1st

A new moon in your sign today gives you another chance to make resolutions regarding your own self and how you show up in the world. Perhaps you wish to do more for your wider community or join a good cause. You may rebel against your family and do something they dislike.

Wednesday 2nd

Today would be a good time to look at what you own, your finances and how you place value on things. You may be in the process of re-evaluating what you really need around you. If it is people you need and not material things, get out there and connect.

Thursday 3rd

Your feelings may be exaggerated today and you are likely to be sharing the love with your tribe. You may also have more self-love and wish to connect with your inner child and soothe old wounds. If you can find a new way of connecting with others, this will help.

Friday 4th

Mercury turns direct today and you may feel a little lightheaded. All that thinking in the small hours may now be put into a practical and workable method. You have touched on what your heart desires and make more effort to go out and get it.

Saturday 5th

Be clear when talking to the opposite sex today. There may be a clash of personal goals. Look after your own agenda now as merging with another might not work today. Take responsibility for yourself and let others work through their own issues. You have no need to take on what isn't yours.

Sunday 6th

The remainder of the weekend may be spent with a high level of change going on. This could be your own views and opinions being challenged and may be rather draining. Let yourself sink into comfortable surroundings this evening as a way to recharge ready for the week.

Monday 7th

Your drive doesn't appear to kick in until late in the day and you may be playing catch up. By evening you could be punishing yourself for a slow start to the week. However, you can make up for it and still have time to do something you love before bed.

Tuesday 8th

There may be a clash of egos today. This is likely to be in your family zone and may make you resentful and stubborn. Talking to someone who understands your personal dreams and visions can distract you from any negativity. Your inner compass calls you to realign with your best self.

Wednesday 9th

Today you see the road ahead, but not how to get there. This may take a while as you need to plan realistic steps towards your dream future. You could be creative about this and make a dream board whereby you add all the ideas you have before sorting them.

Thursday 10th

You may have an irresistible urge to broaden your horizons today, but you are soon deflated or put off. Concentrate on the daily grind for now as this won't get done without your input. Take your responsibilities seriously and be mindful of rules and regulations that keep you on track.

Friday 11th

All you want to do is to dream and plan what you wish to do this year. Listen carefully to any messages that come your way as you may well be receiving your new important mission statement now. What you want and how you feel are in sync today.

Saturday 12th

The celestial lovers are very close in your private sector. This may mean that a secret affair is possible. It may also mean that you are merging both sides of yourself, masculine and feminine, and making strong alliances to help you step out and into the world.

Sunday 13th

You may have a moment of crisis today as you have trouble reconciling a strong sense of independence and solitude. You need people and can't see yourself as a solo traveller. This may not be as bad as you think. It may just be a small part of your life that requires you alone.

Monday 14th

Do you have a last-minute urge to check on something? Follow your instincts as you may have overlooked an important facet of your new mission. Whilst you are learning to love yourself and accept your faults, you may not even notice what has changed or been lovingly released.

Tuesday 15th

Give yourself a hug and promise to check in with your inner child regularly. Old habits and conditioning are being discarded and it may feel strange. Be your own cheerleader now. Look to your romantic partner or close friend to support you as you walk on unfamiliar terrain.

Wednesday 16th

There is a wonderful full moon in your relationship zone today just as Mars and Venus meet up. Take advantage of this energy and do something very special with a loved one. This may mean that your important relationships have reached a new level and you are ready to go deeper together.

Thursday 17th

You may be on cloud nine today and unwilling to come down. The romantic energy continues for you. Surprise yourself and a partner by doing something out of the box. Be rebellious together and go on an unusual date. Forget your duties and have some fun today.

Friday 18th

You can come back down to earth now, because the dreamy energy is actually quite grounding for you. This can mean that what you have been developing under this recent influence has a solid foundation and a good chance of lasting. This is something to build on for the future.

Saturday 19th

This is a good time to talk to a partner. Think of your wildest hopes and dreams. There may be a chance for you to explore them together. A friend or partner may bring something to the mix which you have not considered before but will compliment your plans nicely.

Sunday 20th

Today you might feel a little disappointed with yourself or a partner. You may have a trigger moment which knocks you off balance. This is only a passing phase but is meant to make you slow down and not get too far ahead of yourself. Dream big but stay sensible.

Monday 21st

Your career could be on your mind for the next couple of days Aquarius. You still have the power of that combined male and female energy and you may be able to put it to good use in the workplace. You can be assertive and compassionate, driven and balanced, thinking and feeling.

Tuesday 22nd

An intense and seductive Moon can enrich a love affair or the work you have been doing on yourself. You may be tempted to break a rule to achieve a dream. Is this fair? Who are you trying to deceive? Stick to the harmonising energy at all costs.

Wednesday 23rd

A midweek social with your wider friendship groups may be a good activity today. You desire the benefit of collective wisdom and experience and can learn a lot by getting involved. What is your part in the bigger world? Do you have a role? Would you like to have one?

Thursday 24th

If you have agreed to take part in a group activity, you will need to put your money where your mouth is today. It would be unacceptable for you to let people down or go back on your word now. Do what you promised and keep the faith with your friendship groups.

Friday 25th

You may feel as if your mission, your inner compass and life path have abandoned you. It is not the time for these things. You must learn that there is a time for work, play and for your deep inner work. Get your thinking cap on and do some introspection today.

Saturday 26th

A quiet day will do you some good. Feel into the polarities working inside you. Both your masculine and feminine sides have a right to be expressed and are finding it easy to do so. Note how this feels. Congratulate yourself for doing a little bit of mindfulness.

. . . .

Sunday 27th

This is a lovely day as your emotions are taking everything you have learned recently into account. You may have a new level of understanding of yourself and how you relate to others. Something profound has altered in you. Are you aware of this?

Monday 28th

What may begin as a difficult day becomes something to celebrate. You may have noticed that you have a greater sense of where you are going and what you are leaving behind. You have a newfound confidence which, if you show it to others, will be contagious and everyone will benefit when around you.

MARCH

· · · · · · · · · · · · · · · · · ·

Tuesday 1st

It's possible that you wake up feeling restricted today. You may feel apathetic or simply slow and encumbered. Don't fret too much as this will pass and you get a shot of excitable energy through communicating with others or from young family members. Sudden realisations or breakthroughs are likely today.

Wednesday 2nd

The new moon sees you make goals and aspirations which may be idealistic and unattainable. There is a spiritual side to this which may mean that you seek something outside of the natural world. A yoga or meditation class might suffice. You feel very optimistic this evening. Do something fun.

Thursday 3rd

Great planetary energy allows you to connect with your true north and align all your faculties ready for great change. You may be thinking about a self-improvement course or a group to join to really get in touch with your psyche and understand what makes you tick.

Friday 4th

You are revved up and ready to go! The future is looking bright and you want to be there already. Use this motivating time to make plans, get inspired and seek advice from those who have done similar things. A little forethought will be good in the long run and save corrections later.

Saturday 5th

You have blessings galore today. Mars and Venus are still playing nicely together in your private sector. You may have big ideas today and people will notice how these have lifted you up. You may appear to bounce through the day and brush off any negativity.

Sunday 6th

More luck and love come your way. Mars and Venus have entered your sign together. Could it be that a secret love affair has been revealed and welcomed? This could also be the new you showing your face to the public and putting all you have learned recently to the test. Good luck.

Monday 7th

Things are beginning to grow and develop for you. You have a chance to ground your plans in reality now. Look at what is solid and sustainable. Forget transient things as you will get bored and frustrated. Plant your seeds of inspiration now and tend them well.

Tuesday 8th

You have an intense pull towards your future goals. One lesson you must learn this year is that things don't happen all at once. You must be prepared to do the work in order to reap the results. Your mind may be going crazy with creative or romantic notions today.

Wednesday 9th

You have a rare moment of emotional stability and you almost check yourself. Yes, this is real. There are a lot of planets in your sign which are helping you with love, passion, communication and responsibility. This is a great time for you to promote yourself and your new ventures.

Thursday 10th

Today you may struggle to connect to your dreams. You have
duties to perform before you have a chance to play. The next
few weeks will be intense regarding communications. You may
attach yourself to a new spiritual group or a course of learning.
There is much you desire to learn.

Friday 11th

Maternal figures attract you today as they have what you need.
Familiarity, comfort and security are what you crave now.
This may be as simple as home-cooked food that reminds you
of childhood. There may be a chance to catch up with siblings
and have a nostalgic time together.

Saturday 12th

This weekend may be full of family adventures or get-
togethers. You may need to unwind in the bosom of your tribe
and be that unfiltered child you once were. Everyone has their
roles in families and yours may be to inspire and encourage
others today. Be someone the young ones will look up to.

Sunday 13th

Your inner compass, your true north is shining like a beacon
today. You may feel perfectly at ease sharing your aspirations
with family members or those you meet on a daily basis.
Things are about to change. You may feel a little hesitant, but
this is perfectly natural.

. . . .

Monday 14th

You may come down to earth with a bump today. Your romantic partner may be out-shining you and you don't like it. There may be a clash of egos and resentment will start to build. This is just a blip and not too serious so don't make it any worse.

Tuesday 15th

Again, you could feel challenged or restricted. Right now, you are not happy that you are not getting the attention you desire. Maybe lie low today and think about what you can learn from this situation. Try to be pleased for other people.

Wednesday 16th

A simple day of introspection will do you good. You can be a deep thinker when you need to be, so today is a good day to process some of what you have experienced recently. How might you shine for others' benefit instead of your own? How might you be of service unconditionally?

Thursday 17th

Today has the most uncomfortable energy which will make you sulk, have a tantrum or withdraw. If you feel like this, take the opportunity to spend some time alone doing mundane things such as paperwork or banking. Use your mental faculties to distract you from being too emotional now.

Friday 18th

The full moon may highlight where you need to check yourself and slow down. It may be that you have been running on adrenaline and now need to look at how this has affected your overall health. Try to find a balance that works for you and those you connect with.

Saturday 19th

Your inner harmony returns, and you may have to make an apology or two. You may not like this very much but it's necessary to keep the peace, especially in your family. You can be selfish without thinking about how it affects others. Stay mindful and respectful of those you connect with.

Sunday 20th

The spring equinox occurs today, and this is a great chance to align yourself with the energy of pausing before acting This can be intensely irritating for you as it may feel like a coil ready to spring. However, it's a good practice if you can manage it occasionally.

Monday 21st

Be very careful not to blow your own trumpet too loudly. You may have much to think about and say, and this will come out in a very exaggerated way. There may be jealousy or gossip around, and you should stay away from it. Shock tactics won't work.

Tuesday 22nd

The energy today is volatile and unstable. You may feel restricted and this may cause a lot of tension. If you find that you are looking back at the past with some regret, turn this around and note how far you have come instead. Your journey is more important than the destination.

Wednesday 23rd

Have a chat with yourself and ensure that you are doing what it takes to align with your true north. A pep talk will lift you up and get you back on track. Love relationships are smooth, so keep the lines of communication open and flowing.

Thursday 24th

This is another testing day where your frustrations can almost make you give up hope. You question if you are being too idealistic. There is nothing wrong with getting a reality check as long as you listen to the sound advice you are getting. An elder or a teacher can help today.

Friday 25th

After a trying couple of days, you may find that you have a breakthrough now. Alternatively, you may decide to down tools and go and have some fun instead. Either way, you can use your unusual mind to solve problems or unwind in a unique way. Good luck.

Saturday 26th

Your emotions turn inwards but you resist the need for introspection. Keeping your innermost thoughts to yourself may mean that you are putting on an outward face that is false. Your closest friends may notice this. What might you have overlooked regarding money? Something needs your attention now.

Sunday 27th

Today you feel lighter and brush off negativity. You have a job to do and people need to see the brighter, funny side of you. This doesn't mean that you are free of worry, this will return to you when alone. Communications and plans are enhanced now as you get the go-ahead.

Monday 28th

Emotions may feel like a roller coaster today, but you must learn to flow with them. Challenges may be thrown at you from all sides and you feel as if you are being tested. The Universe is asking you to deal with all sides of your personality.

Tuesday 29th

Take a day to connect or merge with spiritual matters. Yoga or meditation may help you to come back to your centre and feel more stable. You may also like to do something practical such as house cleaning or balancing your finances. A tidy home and business will help to settle you.

Wednesday 30th

Whatever your feelings are when you begin the day, they will get bigger and bigger. You may default to dreaming about unattainable things or you may go out and make an impulse buy. This may make you happy for a short while. Find something that is sustainable instead.

. . . .

Thursday 31st

You are more geared up to make plans today. These may be
inspired by your dreams. There may be a lot of communicating
or short trips to do. Networking is easy now and you enjoy the
pace of the day, as by evening, you feel that you have been
very productive.

APRIL
· · · · · · · · · · · · · · · · · ·

Friday 1st

The new moon today is a great opportunity to set intentions for learning new things. There may be something close to your heart that you have been itching to do. You have the passion and drive to for this. Do all the research now and get the facts together for a new enterprise.

Saturday 2nd

Put yourself first today and do something that makes you feel good. You may be in the spotlight and wish to show off a new look or attitude. This can be inspiring for others. This evening, a little food for the soul will do you good. Family can help.

Sunday 3rd

You may learn something to your advantage today. Listen very carefully to any messages you receive, including those from your own mind. You may be restless, but that energy will help you to come up with something ingenious. You may have a 'eureka!' moment so enjoy it.

Monday 4th

Today may be challenging as you have no wish to start putting down foundations. Instead, you want to run before you can walk. You may feel irritable, blocked and wish you had never thought of this new idea. You may not be kind to yourself today and come across as very childish.

Tuesday 5th

The energy you wake up with will change throughout the day so be patient. At first, you may experience it as a tension waiting to be released. If you can be creative about this, an exercise class or a de-stress therapy may help. Money matters are given a positive boost now.

Wednesday 6th

Use today to research or network, you will be in the right frame of mind to consider all options available to you. This will make you feel good and lift your spirits. Finally, you feel as if you are on the right path rather than still at the starting point.

Thursday 7th

Look at things from all perspectives today. This may be difficult for you but will ultimately be beneficial. You can be too set in your ways about something you wish to do. Romance is easy today, so scoop up a loved one and get cosy this evening.

Friday 8th

Right now, and for some days, your tendency to dream big will consume you. This can be a lovely dreamy time, but you must keep one foot on the ground. You may overdo the luxuries in life or step up and take what is owed to you. Enjoy being on cloud nine.

Saturday 9th

A nurturing moon adds to your blessings today. Your finances may be looking good, but you may be tempted to blow them on an impulse buy. Use this great advantage another way and spend money on making your environment pleasing to you. Then take a well-earned aromatic bath.

Sunday 10th

Partner time is highlighted today, but you may only want it your own way. You may need to have a discussion with a loved one about control issues – and this won't be easy. Conversation styles may be edgy and tense with power struggles showing up. You may experience triggers today.

Monday 11th

That dreamy time is getting more intense now. Self-care, what you feel is valuable to you and finances are all themes for this. You need to be very careful over the next few days regarding where your money goes. You may spend just to spite someone. This is not good.

Tuesday 12th

Hold on tight today as the energy suggests that you may be breaking all the rules and hosting your own revolution. There will be no stopping you getting your own way, and if there is, you will throw a tantrum.

Wednesday 13th

You may still be unwilling to compromise. However, you have calmed down and are putting your mind to other things. Problem-solving or detailed administration can be the best activity for you today. You can excel in getting to the bottom of a problem and this will please you greatly.

Thursday 14th

You may have no time for frivolous activity today, although the pull is there. Your emotions are spent, and you know better than to get wound up again. Is there anything you have overlooked which needs your attention now? This may be something to do with your fitness or outward appearance.

Friday 15th

Your money and values area is packed with planets right now. Take some time to assess and evaluate what feels good to you, what brings you financial security and where you need to merge with others to make your dreams come true. This ethereal energy can bring you a lot of good fortune.

Saturday 16th

The full moon today is highlighting what is in balance in your life. It may be that you have the urge to travel and have not had the time. You may also wish to do some higher education but do not have the funds. Work this balance into your game plan.

Sunday 17th

An intense moon might see you working today. You have the drive and energy to put your mind to career matters. This may be by going deep into an area which has previously evaded you. Use focus and intent to get right to the bottom of a problem.

Monday 18th

There is heavy energy to begin with this week. Emotionally, you are distracted by the promise of greater things and plot how you may get them. Your mind is doing overtime and you may be at risk of being the work gossip or be the one who solves a tricky situation.

. . . .

Tuesday 19th

Reach out to your wider social groups today. Conversations may be difficult but will ultimately help to make a big and necessary change. What can you transform or recycle for the better? You may be encouraged to take up an exercise regime or be told that you need to start one.

Wednesday 20th

Family matters will take your attention for the next month. However, today you may find that you simply can't settle on one job. You may have many on the go at the same time and struggle. Focus on one thing at a time and do it well.

Thursday 21st

You can slow down today and turn inwards. A little introspection and a check-in with your deepest emotions may help you to engage with your outside world better. Time spent on spiritual matters or yoga and meditation will both ground you and lift you to a better viewpoint.

Friday 22nd

The deepest parts of your psyche are screaming for you to take more care of yourself. This includes being real and not acting in denial of things you find difficult to deal with. Your family may help to bring you to a sense of calm and duty, making you pleasantly surprised.

Saturday 23rd

Do you feel a shift happening inside you? Even minor changes can make big differences today. Let go of something you can't change and lighten your load. This may feel strange at first, but you will see the benefits later on. Family discussions can be fun and uplifting today.

Sunday 24th

Your inner rebel wants to come out and play. This may not be a good idea as you may want to do this within your family group and cause some upset. Play by the rules or it will come back and kick you in the face in the future.

Monday 25th

Today it is important that you listen to an elder or a person in authority. You may not like what you hear but this is a big lesson for you to toe the line. It may bruise your ego a little, but you will bounce back and forget about it soon.

Tuesday 26th

Your emotions may be bubbling under the surface and getting ready to blow like a volcano. This is an energy that if you harness it properly, can result in something finally getting done. You need this boost to either get started or complete a long-standing project you might have neglected.

Wednesday 27th

Today you are back to dreaming mode and may be blinkered to reality. This will almost certainly include spending money you may not have in an effort to give yourself a quick fix. Try using it to take care of your body and its needs. Beauty treatment or cooking a favourite meal would suffice.

Thursday 28th

Having a quiet day is recommended. Listen to your inner voice and reconnect sensibly with your true north. You may have more inner work to do than you realise. Family members you trust can offer some good advice and you should take some of this on board.

Friday 29th

Pluto turns retrograde today. This may be the overhaul you
need in your deepest psyche. The next few months may feel
like you are re-working and re-inventing your own story. This
is a great time to go deep and do the hard and sometimes dirty
work to find the pearls hidden below

Saturday 30th

A new moon and solar eclipse will open an unexpected
opportunity for you. Set your roots down carefully and firmly,
and let your direction grow from there. You may have some
good fortune this evening or be feeling very positive about
yourself. Be open to what may come.

MAY

· · · · · · · · · · · · · · · · ·

Sunday 1st

With the help of family and your tribe, you may be able to put your energy into something that is practical yet clever today. This may be a home makeover or a new hairstyle. You have the power to change something and make your home and finances something you can love.

Monday 2nd

You may feel like breaking a few rules today or making an off-the-wall statement. Be your usual unpredictable self and let your imagination go wild. You will justify this to yourself, but others may take more convincing. Get creative and add a splash of random colour to your life.

Tuesday 3rd

If you find that you are sluggish and slow today, just go with it. Slow down and step back. You can't be at full speed all the time. You may need to do more research or have the right conversations with the right people who can cheer you on.

Wednesday 4th

Expect the unexpected today as connections may bring radical changes with them. This might rub against the dreams you have in place for yourself so you will need to have a good think. Don't rule anything out just yet as there may be some gems to find here.

Thursday 5th

Get all your mundane duties done then let yourself be cared for. You may need comfort and familiarity now. There is a chance that you become enlightened by something or a huge bomb blows up leaving you with a blank canvas to work from. Get your genius head on now.

Friday 6th

Your creative skills know no bounds today. Love and romance are highlighted, and you may be able to coax a lover into your cosy spot to snuggle under the duvet with ice-cream. If talking into the small hours is your thing, this can be achieved too. Have fun with it.

Saturday 7th

Use caution and check on your finances today. Something that needs urgent attention may surface for you to deal with. Avoid big purchases now. The romantic vibe continues as you both have a lot to say and find out about each other. There may be some healthy competition between you.

Sunday 8th

There is a lot of fiery and passionate energy available to you today. Just be sure to use it wisely and not get burnt. If you aren't careful you may be in for a nasty surprise which rocks your happy boat. Let a partner have their say and don't try hogging the limelight.

Monday 9th

Today may be difficult as you may not be playing fair. Your ruler, Saturn, is asking that you be reminded of personal boundaries in your intimate relationships. You want all the pleasure and the recognition. How about letting your partner shine for a while? Let them have their turn.

Tuesday 10th

Mercury turns retrograde today. This will affect your love and family relationships most. Over the next three weeks, you must take extra care to be kind, honest, patient and clear. Do all the usual checks now. Back up devices, double check travel plans and refrain from committing yourself to anything.

Wednesday 11th

Luck will enter your communications and planning now as Jupiter bounces into this area. Watch out for excitement in your family and home today. This may come from unlikely sources or may simply be a party of some kind. You may feel slow or fuzzy-headed by evening.

Thursday 12th

Today you may feel the effect of Mercury retrograde. Long-distance communications and travel may be misunderstood or delayed. Check that people you are dealing with have the same facts as you. Romantic endeavours will need more effort today so prepare to do your part and not let your partner do all the work.

Friday 13th

You may be a little selfish today Aquarius. You see the road ahead and want to travel it immediately. It's possible that you wave goodbye to someone who is not yet ready for your departure. Think twice before you embark on a solo adventure which may be fake.

Saturday 14th

Your energy and drive are still pumping in the direction of the unknown. You need to get a reality check and see where you are headed and not leave everything to chance. There are people waiting in the wings who care about you and your unique ways.

Sunday 15th

You simply will not be told today. Although you may be treading on precarious ground, you feel invincible. Remember that pride comes before a fall. If you can't see your true north ahead of you, then it isn't your path. Retreat now before you lose your way.

Monday 16th

A full moon and lunar eclipse forces you to see the error of your ways. You must backtrack slowly and discard any false promises you have picked up along the way. Your friends and loved ones welcome you back and you are humbled. The time has come to put your energy in the right direction.

Tuesday 17th

You now understand the value of listening to others with more experience. Going off on a whim doesn't always win you any favours. Your social groups can help you to restore your faith and shine your armour ready for the next and proper round of your journey.

Wednesday 18th

Today you should rest as much as you can. Some time alone
to process recent events would be a good activity. Your dreams
and visions may be out of sight, but this lets you concentrate
on matters closer to home. When you are ready, your personal
energy and true north are perfectly aligned.

Thursday 19th

As you may know, you have just released an old habit which
no longer serves you. You can look at things with fresh eyes
and more wisdom. You have surprised yourself and made the
first steps on the most important journey of all. The journey to
your best self.

Friday 20th

Do not get dragged into other people's plans today as they
are likely to go wrong in a big way. Stay in solitude and
contemplate your own personal growth and change. You may
come out of this zone with a plan that will work better for you.

Saturday 21st

Take today one minute at a time and try not to step out of line.
The Sun is shining on your romantic and creative pursuits,
and any small hiccup will be glaringly obvious today. Mercury
is involved, so ensure that your communications are clear and
precise. There is no room for being vague today.

Sunday 22nd

Everything you do today is being observed. You may act out
of character and this will come back to haunt you. Lie low if
you find it impossible to be good. Watch what you say as this
can come across as very self-centred and ego-driven if you
aren't careful.

Monday 23rd

Take some time today to go over your bank balance, there may be something you have overlooked which needs attention now. You may also notice a last-minute effort to connect or make contact with people on the same path. A late yoga or exercise class would be good.

Tuesday 24th

Try to fix on your true north today as everything else around you seems unstable. If you can, stay home and look at what gives you joy and what doesn't. Maybe a good spring clean or a decluttering session is in order. Is there anything you can upcycle now?

Wednesday 25th

You will find that your communications are far more assertive now and this will help you to plan effectively for the near future. Get out there and learn something new which you can add to your skillset. You may feel like discarding any progress so far, but think twice.

Thursday 26th

It would be useful if you could play by the rules today. Take your responsibilities seriously and know your own limits. You may feel limitless most of the time, but this isn't true. Everyone has their boundaries and you need to get to grips with yours a little more.

Friday 27th

Today is one of those days where you fail to see where you may be under stress or strain and carry on regardless. The more you soldier on, the more you run yourself down. If you notice this at all, take a step back and lighten your load. Self-care is essential.

Saturday 28th

Love and harmony are the objectives today. This may play out within your family of origin. There is a sense of instability which may unsettle some but if you are clever and use your unique ways of thinking, you can restore peace and make family members happy again.

Sunday 29th

The future lies ahead of you but today you seem unable to touch it. Your energy and drive may be larger than usual, and this makes you reach for the unattainable. Know that you can't have everything and especially not today. Be more realistic in your goals.

Monday 30th

A new moon and solar eclipse may give you a few reveals today. Love and romance or your creative endeavours are featured now. Might you now see an ending of something the lunar eclipsed opened up? Emotions may be exaggerated so be aware of this when dealing with people who are closest to you.

Tuesday 31st

If all you do today is your mundane duties and messaging, then so be it. Keep your head down and be submissive as your true north is nowhere to be seen. There is nothing you can do about it, so pay attention to your daily duties instead.

JUNE
· · · · · · · · · · · · · · · · · ·

Wednesday 1st

Pay attention to your health today. You may feel run down
and need to take things slower. Delegate duties if you can
and nurture yourself with food or company you enjoy. Your
intuition will be your guide if you stop and listen to it. Being
around maternal figures may help.

Thursday 2nd

You may surprise yourself with how protective you can be
today. Family members need the closeness you can provide and
so do you. This may feel unproductive but is beneficial for your
overall wellbeing. Pull together with family members and offer
mutual support and encouragement. A home-cooked family
meal would be great.

Friday 3rd

Mercury is direct again. Give yourself some breathing space
before rushing into anything now. Intimate conversations
with loved ones may reveal that you are loved more than you
know. Let yourself look forward to a weekend with a romantic
partner and schedule in some fun, play and laughter.

Saturday 4th

Your planetary ruler, Saturn, turns retrograde now. This will
mean that you have a very important lesson to learn regarding
how you see the world. Prepare for some hold-ups or a
humbling of your opinions. Maturity will be the theme. You
may be levelling up to a new you.

Sunday 5th

Today you may feel the first lessons from Saturn. Your love-life may experience some hiccups where you realise you may have crossed a boundary. Pouring your heart out to a partner may help, but you must be discreet and let them stay private if they wish to. Respect that they may not think like you.

Monday 6th

You may have a turn-around of thinking today. It's possible that you push the boat out to make a partner feel comfortable in your presence. This may come across as gushing or people-pleasing so try not to overdo it. Offer your services but remember not to cross the line.

Tuesday 7th

Challenges may surface within your creative pursuits. Maybe you are just not enjoying a project anymore. Look to your roots and remember what you used to enjoy as a child. This may help you to have a brief time of unfiltered play and experimentation. Messy play is always fun.

Wednesday 8th

You can't seem to catch your dreams today and may feel a little fuzzy-headed or frustrated. Turn your attention to something which requires brain work. Maybe you need to check finances and balance your books. Look for old subscriptions or accounts that need clearing. You may find some hidden funds.

Thursday 9th

In your heart, you wish to spread your wings and fly but you simply don't have the physical energy. Allow yourself some downtime and do some reading or researching about other cultures. You may sigh and regret not having visited many places, but watching documentaries or reading will help.

Friday 10th

Something doesn't feel quite right today. You desire to make changes or to drag up past problems and revisit them. This is only good if you intend to learn from them or heal wounds. Talking to family members may bring up past hurts but can be handled well.

Saturday 11th

Familial love may be bursting at the seams today. There is volatile energy, but this is mixed with high levels of compassion and harmony. A long-standing disagreement or grudge may be dealt with once and for all and everyone will breathe a sigh of relief. This is a day of many group hugs.

Sunday 12th

The past has worked its way into the present. Although you may have put grievances behind you there may still be some jealousy or hidden knowledge surrounding it. It is vital that you get this out into the open today. It is time to do the responsible thing now.

Monday 13th

You are emotionally inclined to give your energy to your friends and social groups today. You may wish to sound off in a place where you will not feel judged. Do you feel your creative juices stirring? A new and vibrant project brews in your mind.

Tuesday 14th

Today's full moon lets you see how much you have grown this year. Social groups may have been more help to you than you realise. You may have learned about other cultures, religions and philosophies, or made friends from around the world. Celebrate diversity today.

Wednesday 15th

A quiet day attracts you. You may simply wish to be alone with your thoughts or catch up on activities you would normally do. It's not that you are anti-social, but you have run out of steam for anything new right now. Have a day for yourself and tackle personal goals.

Thursday 16th

You may still be feeling the need for a slower pace today. Close family members will understand and may even help you to enjoy your solitude. Self-control is important to you now as you evaluate recent days and work on a new and improved way of dealing with old habits and conditioning.

Friday 17th

Your bounce returns and you are ready for the weekend. Whatever you choose to do today will be enhanced. This may also involve going over the top a little so be careful. One drink leads to another. The all-you-can-eat buffet appeals – but you may regret it.

Saturday 18th

A big red light appears to halt your progress today. You may come up against many challenges within your family and you will be asked to step up your game. It's likely that you will act like a small child and have a major tantrum. This is not a good look.

Sunday 19th

In an effort to please yourself, you may go out and spend too much today. Luxury items are within your grasp, but this is just a short-term fix for the sulky mood you are in. Think twice before spending money. If you are indecisive about something, leave it there, it's not for you.

Monday 20th

You may be wondering where your true north has gone. If you look carefully, this is the best time of the month to connect to it. However, you may be seeing it through a red mist, and it is distorted. Try to clear your head before anchoring onto it.

Tuesday 21st

It is the summer solstice today. This longest day will give you the chance to evaluate how the year has gone so far. You may feel that productivity has only just begun. Your big heart may be reaching out to others and connecting to everything outside of yourself.

Wednesday 22nd

Your drive and energy seem to be on full speed today. You put all of your heart and soul into whatever you do. This may make you single-minded but in a good way. You will certainly get what you want today and maybe a wish comes true.

Thursday 23rd

Venus is about to brighten up your love life now. You may have found your muse and your creativity is overflowing. This may feel like a race to the finish line, but you are enjoying the view too much to slow down. What have you just left behind or transformed?

Friday 24th

Your heart may still be pumping with adrenaline as you spill out ideas, words and love. Be very careful that you are not being too much for some people. You are ready to explode, and this could go two ways. Make sure it is productive or things could get very messy.

Saturday 25th

You may be learning one of Saturn's lessons today. Where might you need to assume more responsibility within your family group? Have you ignored the advice of elders and gone down your own unpredictable path? A different perspective might help you to re-align and get things right.

Sunday 26th

The energy is right for a romantic, sexy day today. You could be messaging a lover or chatting through the night. This may be someone new who you wish to get to know better, but you are still in the dating stages and being somewhat naïve or starstruck. Keep it real.

Monday 27th

Whatever is in your heart will come out of your mouth today. Are you sure you are ready for this? It would be advisable to curb your impulse to spill everything about yourself. This energy may also produce some great art, music or poetry. Exercise caution and be mindful of boundaries.

Tuesday 28th

Neptune, your true north, turns retrograde today. You may go through a period of disillusionment and disappointment now. The way to deal with this is to always keep one foot on the ground. Practising grounding activities or getting outdoors more will be helpful. As will yoga or meditation.

Wednesday 29th

Today there is a new moon which is a good time to set goals and intentions regarding your mundane duties and how you are of service to others. Perhaps you need to spend more time being selfless or looking out for younger members of the family. You may need to protect your own boundaries more.

Thursday 30th

You are more than willing to help out and do your bit. However, this is short-lived and when you have had enough you tend to retreat. Try to see things from another's point of view. Have you done enough or are you just paying them lip service?

JULY

....

Friday 1st

Plans for the weekend may include your beloved. Make the most of this lovely energy which enables you to whisper words of love and make beautiful plans together. You may reveal more about yourself today and a loved one will be eager to listen. Hear them out too.

Saturday 2nd

Today may be challenging but can also be productive if you listen to your urges. You are conscious of not repeating old patterns and wish to disrupt the status quo, breaking free from tradition. This is great if you take care to remember that there are two of you involved.

Sunday 3rd

Chatting and expressing yourself can be playful today. Be sure to play nicely and abide by the rules. There is a chance you may feel restricted in some way, but this is probably a childhood habit of expecting your own way too much. Take it down a notch this afternoon.

Monday 4th

You may not feel as if your needs are getting met and your ego may take a bashing. It is crucial that you express yourself and be assertive if you need to. There may be someone you have neglected to catch up with, do it now Aquarius.

Tuesday 5th

Good food and company may make a weeknight special. You may have an intense time of loving or dating which reaches a new level of caring and devotion. Your own personal dreams don't matter much today as you are content with the connection you are getting from someone special.

Wednesday 6th

Today you may feel off balance and wonder why. This may be an uncomfortable feeling but will soon pass. If you tip this balance in favour of selfish needs, you may find yourself getting a ticking off from someone in authority. Talk it out and learn where you went wrong.

Thursday 7th

Your mind may be settled by creative and romantic pursuits today. Harmony is restored and you could feel flirtatious. A mature approach is essential now as your ruler Saturn is asking that you take the responsible road and own your insecurities. Don't avoid them or project them onto a loved one.

Friday 8th

The energy today can be secretive or sexy. It will depend on how you play it. Stay away from control games and find a middle ground to look at what is safe and what is risky. Talk about your comfort zones with a loved one and give total respect to theirs.

Saturday 9th

Old secrets and loves may haunt you today. You may have shared something which is now triggering feelings you would rather not deal with. Restlessness may turn into volatile behaviour if you are not careful. Family matters may come to a head.

Sunday 10th

Your inner compass may give you a nudge now and you come back to your personal dreams and visions. A different perspective makes you sit up and look at the world through new eyes. Something has to change today, and you feel ruthless enough to do it. Decluttering would be a good activity. A social event would be nice too.

Monday 11th

Your loyalties may be split today as your social groups are calling you as well as your love life. It would be helpful to check in with your groups in the evening as there may be something you hear to your advantage. End the day with some you-time.

Tuesday 12th

A boost of energy will help you process your inner thoughts. You may begin solving a problem that is hindered by your need to be seen as successful. Let something go and stop being so hard on yourself. Spend some time alone this evening if you can.

Wednesday 13th

A full moon may throw a spotlight on something from your unconscious. You may wish to work this through with a trusted friend. Your head and heart are not in sync and you would benefit from an unbiased second opinion. It is not as big a problem as you think.

Thursday 14th

You may have a sleepless night as your emotional self is churning up all sorts from your psyche. This is essential to the healing process and needs to come up. You may feel that all eyes are on you, making you vulnerable and perhaps a little temperamental.

Friday 15th

Listen to good advice today as it will aid in processing old thoughts that no longer help. If you feel stuck between past and future, stay in the present and simply enjoy the moment. This isn't easy for you, as you may want to rebel or run away.

Saturday 16th

Listen to what your body is saying. Are you taking care of yourself? You may wish to do something today which makes you feel loved, nurtured and protected. Home-cooked foods and maternal figures will help you so reach out to someone who can offer you these delights. Buy yourself a treat too.

Sunday 17th

Spending today on a love or creative project will be fruitful. You may find that you have another piece of the puzzle and that you have more to learn. Discoveries of all sorts are possible now. Your family may provide some fun or a day of high energy.

Monday 18th

Your heart re-aligns with your true north but be careful that you are not looking through rose-coloured glasses. There may be an illusion there. Don't give out too much of yourself as this may tire you. Resentment may build if you feel that the balance of give and take is off.

Tuesday 19th

Your health needs a check-up now. You may have neglected some issues and they have now resurfaced for attention. Watch what you say today as you may find yourself backtracking on a commitment or promise and that won't look good. Say what you mean with kindness and respect.

Wednesday 20th

Watch out for control issues or people asking too much of you. This is another day where you may feel that you are giving too much of yourself. Try to reduce your mundane duties or delegate some to another person. You may be too soft and being taken advantage of right now.

Thursday 21st

Romance is highlighted today. It may be less about talking and more about sensual activity. Getting intimate with a lover may show you just how much you can protect each other. Sharing a tasty meal in evocative surroundings will add spice to your love life and soften things up.

Friday 22nd

Hold on to your hat today. This may be the time to take a leap of faith and commit to someone special. Together you may do something unusual or share dreams that the two of you can now begin to implement. The Sun moves into your relationship area to help with this.

Saturday 23rd

You are still in a romantic frame of mind. Today may bring you some luck or simply enhance the good feeling you both have. Conversations are easy and optimistic. You may feel a change happening in your psyche. A healthy trigger has shifted an old, outdated pattern.

Sunday 24th

Enjoy the remainder of the weekend with some fun and laughter. You may wish to be childlike and unfiltered. Laughter is the best medicine now and will remind you that this doesn't happen often enough. Set yourself free and go exploring with your perfect travel partner. Where might you end up?

Monday 25th

The working week may dampen your spirits as you come back to the daily grind. You may feel like rebelling and taking a sick day just so you can stay in the glow of the moment. Unfortunately, this isn't possible so you will just have to knuckle down and get on with it.

Tuesday 26th

Your heart is filled with love and harmony, but your mind keeps referring you back to your work. You may also be distracted by family and your home today. Be mindful of what you say as you could unwittingly voice your reluctance to be a team player.

Wednesday 27th

A little midweek fun is up for grabs today. Sneaking away from your obligations may feel rebellious but is harmless and you can get away with it. You could stay up late tonight and chat into the early hours. You are in a dreamy mood and just a bit unrealistic.

Thursday 28th

A hot new moon in your relationship area will allow you and a loved one to set shared goals and intentions. Make sure you say your piece, or you could be swept away with the wishes of another. Jupiter turns retrograde so the coming months may feel a little heavier.

Friday 29th

Today has many challenges so breathe deeply. You may feel pushed and pulled between family and work obligations. At the same time, you may discover that Jupiter is asking you to slow down and stay closer to home for a while. Those big ideas will have to wait for a better time.

Saturday 30th

You are sure to say whatever is on your mind now. Your lover may appreciate your honesty but do check that what you have to say is true, kind and respectful or you could be heading for trouble. Getting deeper with a lover may mean talking about difficult topics with them.

Sunday 31st

An elder or teacher may pull you aside and tell you that you have gone too far. Alternatively, it may be you who is feeling uncomfortable and exposed. It's possible that you have a moment of crisis and are unsure of what to do next. Stop, breathe and think.

AUGUST

Monday 1st

You may be running headlong into trouble today. This energy
may mean that you will be prone to little accidents or bust-ups
so take caution. Alternatively, you may go off on a tangent,
believing that you have found a new path. Stop and check all
the tiny details first.

Tuesday 2nd

What huge changes are you making today? This may not be
right for you as it's fuelled by unstable energy. You may find
that you backtrack and check yourself, as you may have felt
too vulnerable once you have fully realised what you are doing.
Keep yourself safe and protected.

Wednesday 3rd

Your family will thank you today as you are extra-protective
and nurturing. Young people may need your advice or your
shoulder to cry on. This is also a good day to show that you are
serious about your obligations to them. Restore the balance of
giving and receiving today.

Thursday 4th

Intense emotions may mean that you put your mind to your
career and do your very best. You can go deep into a problem
or really go to extremes with productivity today. Sharing with
a lover or work partner can also be intriguing and get your
detective-like mind doing overtime.

Friday 5th

You may struggle with your ego today and believe that you need to do more to get more. The past may come back into your awareness and remind you of the skills you once utilised. Tantrums are possible as you break free from expected behaviour and do your own thing.

Saturday 6th

Get a grip today and slow down. Emotional energy can blindside you into illusions and take your focus from your daily duties. It's possible that you find more work to do on your deepest self and this annoys you. Do something grounding or physical today, and reach out to friends this evening.

Sunday 7th

A little coaxing by maternal figures may help you to unwind and spend some time with home comforts. You may have a mind to travel or learn something new, but you are unsure what. Make sure that you don't take on another fruitless project which you will abandon later on.

Monday 8th

Your inner compass is eluding you and this is frustrating. Hold on to what you know and what is around you for now. Tackling your responsibilities and lessening your workload will be good. There may be things that need completing – and now is a good time to focus on them.

Tuesday 9th

Today may be difficult for you as you have material from your psyche popping up and upsetting you. You may be wishing that it would all get buried again and not have to be dealt with. Mothers, caring, nurturing and being of service will all be on your mind right now.

Wednesday 10th

You may feel incredibly miserable today as feelings of inadequacy surface. You may wonder if you are good enough and lovable. Feeling sorry for yourself won't change anything. You must notice why you have been triggered and find a way to heal. Be patient and kind to yourself.

Thursday 11th

Venus, the planet of love enters your relationship area today. Prepare to get romantic more often. You may find that this influence harmonises or smooths out bumps in your one to one relationships. If you feel irritable with family members, stay silent as this is not worth a fight.

Friday 12th

There is a full moon in your sign today. You may feel that the spotlight is on you but not in a positive way. Quite the opposite, you may feel that all your little imperfections are showing. Remember that nobody is perfect and that you are loved for who you are.

Saturday 13th

Talking doesn't seem to help today. Are you reluctant to see outside yourself? You may be checking and double-checking little details as a way to avoid looking inwards. If you have a spiritual practice, try connecting and finding your centre of calm. Yoga and meditation might help.

Sunday 14th

Why not use today to switch off and give yourself quality alone time. You may do a little work on yourself without it causing too much pain. You may not even realise you are doing it. Be good to yourself and seek your true north. Get re-aligned and ready for the week ahead.

Monday 15th

You may be drawn to connect with a loved one today, and love messages will add cheer to your day. It may surprise you to know just how easily you can talk to your partner if you remember that they are human too. Reach out and make some plans together.

Tuesday 16th

Your mood lifts and you may find that you laugh a lot with family members. You recall what it was like growing up and may revert back to unfiltered childhood habits with siblings or parents. If you were the family rebel, you will see traits of that side of you again.

Wednesday 17th

An easy day of food and company you love will be satisfying. This may not include a romantic partner and you will need to reassure them that this is not personal. You desire to hunker down under the duvet and chat to relatives whilst eating ice-cream or another favourite food.

Thursday 18th

You may be playful or in the mood for intimacy today. Whichever it is it will be packed with energy and can be invigorating. This lift helps to move you out of a slump you have felt yourself in. Get moving, make love, dance, do exercise or declutter your home.

Friday 19th

This is a good day for implementing a change or trying something connected to your true north. Perhaps you have an opportunity to make money or invest in a scheme. Look at what is most valuable and beneficial in the long term and cast quick fixes to one side.

Saturday 20th

Your emotions and sex drive are on the same side today so you may have a passionate weekend. All the signs are there for you to enjoy a clandestine meeting or a seductive time with someone special. Talking, laughing and loving are the flavours of the weekend so make the most of it.

Sunday 21st

It's possible that you have had too much of a good thing and the weekend has already come to a halt. You may feel disillusioned as you see the faults in someone. Talk this through as you may be at fault for not being very realistic.

Monday 22nd

You must put something right today regarding your relationships. You may feel sorry for rocking the boat. It's hard for you to apologise and own up to being in the wrong. Be humble and not gushing as this will make things worse. Talking may trigger old habits, so think before speaking.

Tuesday 23rd

Decide to put your partner first for a change and this will make a huge difference in your relationship. Look at all the things you can do for them unconditionally. You may see many benefits from this and reach a new, deeper more intimate level with your loved one.

Wednesday 24th

Uranus turns retrograde today in your family area so prepare for things to get a little crazy. You may think about breaking free and rebelling against the expected norm. This will be a time for you to look at new ways of doing traditional things or breaking from tradition altogether.

Thursday 25th

This is a challenging day where you may find it difficult to keep to your promise of putting someone else's needs first. You may be stubborn or outspoken. Your lover may see you like a spoilt child right now, do you really want that? Have some time out if necessary.

Friday 26th

Negotiations are possible now, so have a good long think if you wish to jeopardise a relationship for the sake of getting your own way. You may have to retreat if you are unable to come to a resolution. Don't throw a tantrum as it will not be appreciated.

Saturday 27th

A new moon is your perfect opportunity to have tactic talks and discuss how you can serve in an equal manner with a partner. However, the energy is unstable, and you may not get the results you desire. Put things down on paper, go away and come back in a few days with fresh eyes.

Sunday 28th

You should step up and do the right thing today. Saturn, your ruler is looking at how you deal with matters of unconditional love. Is it all about you or do you have the ability to step out with a partner as a formidable pair?

Monday 29th

It may have taken a while, but your heart and head are finally on speaking terms. You may achieve a sense of harmony and balance today but only if you are passionate about doing the right thing. You may be able to see a future that is loving and nurturing.

Tuesday 30th

Take it easy today as the energy is oppressive and may weigh you down. This is external and has nothing to do with your recent upsets. Do something that involves higher learning, other cultures or religions and you may find that you get through the day a little easier.

Wednesday 31st

Your sense of duty returns, and you find that a milestone has been reached. Give yourself a reward for letting an old and outdated version of you go. This may have been one of Saturn's lessons for you this year and you have passed with flying colours. Well done.

SEPTEMBER
· · · · · · · · · · · · · · · · · ·

Thursday 1st
The past attracts you today and you may be reminiscing or yearning for a time when things were easier. This may, in fact, help you to bring back a skill set which you have left behind. What old ways of working can you adopt once more in the workplace?

Friday 2nd
You may be disillusioned or disappointed with the way you have been brought up. There is a stubborn streak to you today which hinders your progress. Look at how you present yourself to the world and be mature about any changes that are needed. You may just need a tweak or two.

Saturday 3rd
Travel and connecting with old friends may be on your mind now. You may feel that you have neglected people and make promises to yourself to correct that soon. Social groups and lovers divide your time, and this can be tricky to manage. You may feel drained trying to please all.

Sunday 4th
Venus spends her last day in your relationship area. It is important that you have quality time with a partner now and really hear what they have to say. This may be a make or break time and you will need to be a compassionate listener.

Monday 5th

Retreat and have some private time today. You may wish to be alone with your thoughts and process recent days in your own time. Just be careful that your own bias doesn't get in the way. Be as open as possible to sharing and caring for the special people in your life.

Tuesday 6th

You are much brighter now and feel more positive about your future. You may find that something from your psyche is easily healed and allows you to grow. Look at what you hold dear and what you value most. Self-care is included now too. Be kind to yourself.

Wednesday 7th

The Moon in your sign makes you bouncy and ready for the outside world. You have a charm that is addictive to others. Ensure that this is genuine and not a way to put on a mask and avoid real issues. Romance is highlighted as you are outgoing and cheerful.

Thursday 8th

If you feel stuck, stand in that space and be the observer. This is just a phase and will pass soon. Moments like these allow you to check-in with yourself and make sure everything is in working order. Act in a responsible, mature manner and all will be well.

Friday 9th

You have a desire to connect and get to know someone on a deeper level. However, this may conflict with your own needs. Mercury turns retrograde tomorrow, so make all the necessary checks now, especially where long-distance travel is concerned. Work or research needs to be checked before being submitted.

Saturday 10th

A full moon will show you where you have been gathering your resources, seeking spirituality and a higher love. You may see a result or completion of these issues. You can check in with your true north now and see the way forward. This may be very emotional for you.

Sunday 11th

Clear conversation is key today. You may have a lot to say, learn or discuss but may find difficulty in expressing yourself. There is a possibility that you get into arguments or involved in gossip. You may even be blowing your own trumpet, and this will gain disapproval.

Monday 12th

Romantic and sexual advances may be made today. You have just the right amount of interest and energy to have some fun with a partner. Creative pursuits may get a boost if there is something you need to complete. Be mindful of crossing personal boundaries, stay safe and have fun.

Tuesday 13th

Old thoughts or habits may surface to be cleaned out. You may not succeed in this today, but they will stay in your awareness for a while. Put this on your 'to do' list for another time. You may wish to spend quiet time with family and feel your family roots now.

Wednesday 14th

A feeling of comfort and security allows you to be of service to others willingly. You may feel satisfied that you have been of help today. Restless energy may keep you awake but this could also be that you have new ideas or have finally found a solution to a problem.

Thursday 15th

Today you may acquire an understanding of how your true north, your destiny and your inner mind work together. You see the need to make room for new growth and may begin to work on what has surfaced for healing recently. Prioritise achievable goals and discard unrealistic ones.

Friday 16th

A challenging day where you may not see eye to eye with a partner. This can be frustrating but there is no point in pushing it. Give both of you time out to calm down and re-connect when the mood has lifted. You may be resentful of the time taken up by this.

Saturday 17th

Your temper may get the better of you today, so be careful. Love relationships will feel this the most. You may feel lost at sea as nothing is stable enough for you to grasp right now. This phase will pass, so concentrate on mundane jobs to get you through the day.

Sunday 18th

You may stay under the duvet today as you are not prepared to be attacked and have no energy to retaliate. This is probably the best thing for you. Take a day of rest doing the things which feed your soul. Don't be forced out of your comfort zone.

Monday 19th

Today is easier and more productive. You may find that family relationships and finances are the themes you need to work with today. Look at what you own and what you share with others. Gentle energy will help this to go well and you need not worry.

Tuesday 20th

You could be extra emotional today. Your heart is yearning for
harmony, but your restlessness and natural Aquarian habits
want to break free. You may feel torn between two different
actions and feel rushed into deciding. Connect with a lover this
evening and offload your worries.

Wednesday 21st

Plans with a partner are being made, but remember that
Mercury is retrograde, so don't commit to anything just yet.
You may have a sense of urgency or have ideas that are too big
and unrealistic. Slim things down to an achievable level and
wait to set them in stone later.

Thursday 22nd

It's possible that your energy erupts into a mini tantrum today.
You may feel blocked and restricted and will not like this very
much. Your partner may see a side to you that is not to their taste
so be very careful how you act today. Be genuine but be respectful.

Friday 23rd

Today is all about achieving balance. How much do you do
for others? How much do they do for you? Are you taking the
greater load upon yourself? Spend time today being still and
looking at both sides. You may feel pressured into discussing
things you find uncomfortable.

Saturday 24th

Your dreams and visions appear futile now. You may be
disheartened and totally off-centre. Finances may be an issue
here so time spent looking at your bank balance may help to
bring you back into alignment with your inner compass. Try
not to make hasty decisions about your love life today.

Sunday 25th

Emotions may feel like a roller coaster as the day goes by. You may wake up feeling inspired and dreamy. That may turn around later. A new moon suggests that you make goals and intentions to restore harmony and do something which taxes your brain. Higher education may call you.

Monday 26th

Be very careful what words of love you speak as they may not be received the way you wish. You may also come across as ridiculous or make promises you have no intention of keeping. Your feelings lead you to commit to something which you will abandon soon after.

Tuesday 27th

Today it is important that you think twice before making any great changes. These will be permanent and can't be undone. This could also be that you have moved on to a deeper level in a relationship and are fearful of where this will take you. You may not be ready.

Wednesday 28th

Put your mind to work and use your intense focus to get through the day. This will blind you from stuff that is churning around in your psyche for now. Know that it isn't going away, but that you have more urgent things to deal with such as your career.

Thursday 29th

You are drawn back to the past today. This could be an ex-lover or something else you still have deep feelings for. This may be on your mind all day until you finally have time to deal with it. Your family environment may feel your anguish and try to help.

Friday 30th

You have a desire to get out and have some fun this weekend. Making plans with your wider social groups can give you the boost you need. Re-connect with long-distance friends too. You may also enjoy watching television about foreign countries, philosophies and religions to get your travel bug going.

OCTOBER

Saturday 1st

Communications may go awry today so don't hit send before you check a message. This is a frustrating day for getting things done and connecting with your path. Use the time to have some light-hearted pleasure without committing to anything too heavy or draining. Feelings may be misunderstood if expressed to the wrong people.

Sunday 2nd

Mercury is direct now and you may have a startling epiphany about your personal path. This may also involve seeing things from a new perspective. You will have time to adjust to this and go back over something that has evaded you. Alone time will help clear your thoughts.

Monday 3rd

You begin the working week with a sense of satisfaction. There is excitement within your family so expect a few surprises. Your tribe may pull together to make something happen or to pull apart an outdated way of being. A home makeover could be the project you are all involved in.

Tuesday 4th

Changes are happening for you. You may have an emotional investment here and be unsure of how you feel. Let this happen organically as by evening you may see the benefits. Your sense of justice may be rattled but will be balanced out if you think things through before acting.

Wednesday 5th

You may need to halt progress and evaluate things so far. This is not a bad thing as it will enable you to see where you may have been too impatient and chosen badly. You may be asked to step up and own your responsibilities. Put your money where your mouth is.

Thursday 6th

Today the energy is relatively gentle, and you may find that you enter a dreamy frame of mind. You may also feel cut off from reality. Take off the rose-tinted glasses and dream by all means, but keep one foot on the ground. Make sure you don't overspend today.

Friday 7th

If you listen very carefully, you may get a message or two from your inner voice. This may appear as critical and you are doing yourself a disservice. Find the voice that is celebrating the work you have done on your triggers and traumas and reward yourself for your efforts.

Saturday 8th

You are re-aligned with your inner compass now. This will always fluctuate as you have mundane duties to get on with as well as your own personal growth. Your head and heart are not in sync today, so concentrate on one or the other. This evening you may think more clearly.

Sunday 9th

A full moon in your communications area will show how you have made plans and followed or abandoned them. You may now see that you are prone to taking on too much without considering the longevity of your plans. Pluto turns direct and will help to make change more permanent.

Monday 10th

You are driven to move forward with a romance or creative project now. You need to have your voice heard and can be too boisterous and assertive. Slow down, charging in without all the facts will only muddle things up. What is so urgent that you risk a knockback?

Tuesday 11th

Your inquiring mind is very active now. You may wish to look at a course of higher education in something that fascinates you. Broadening your mind or reading around a new topic may help to balance and focus your intent. You may have a calling to travel today.

Wednesday 12th

Get on the right side of someone in authority such as a boss or spiritual leader. You may be challenging this person or asking questions to deepen your knowledge. However, you may be so keen to learn that you are pushing triggers or crossing boundaries. Take it one step at a time.

Thursday 13th

Catching up with a loved one may bring fun and laughter today. Conversations may be quirky or deep. Both are good and will be satisfying. You may be more optimistic and your creativity will be boundless. Explore all your options and see if you can find ones you hadn't previously considered.

Friday 14th

Your ruler, Saturn, may be showing you another lesson today. This will be about emotions and desires. You can't always get what you want, no matter how much you fawn and coax someone. Find the middle ground and make a compromise.

Saturday 15th

Today you may be lost in illusion or simply on cloud nine with a partner. Your sexual energy is high, and you wish to connect with your partner in a way that is both sensual and mutually protective. Get all your provisions and lock both of you away from the outside world.

Sunday 16th

Comfort and security are what you crave. It is time to assess the value of a relationship and what you can both bring to it. Who looks after who? Are you both rowing the boat? Do you feel as if you are doing all the work? Talk about this with ease.

Monday 17th

You may feel triggered today and will need to do some work on this. How does your personal safety impact on your need for control? This may be your ego talking and if so, this is a superficial need and one you can do without. Self-protection may be exaggerated now.

Tuesday 18th

Important relationships are a big issue. You desire to be seen in the spotlight and this may conflict with your partner's needs. Your self-expression may not do you any favours today as you will be unfiltered and say exactly what you mean. This may not be kind or respectful.

Wednesday 19th

You may have to come face to face with your own limitations today. This will not be easy for you, but you must remember that there are people who can help. There is no need to talk about it as your closest friends will simply know and offer you the support you need.

Thursday 20th

Mars and Venus give you a helping hand. Harmony may be restored and your passion for love and creativity burn again. It's possible that you have stepped up another notch on your personal path and have become more humble. This evening you are willing to return favours.

Friday 21st

Enjoy a day with easy energy. This is a rare chance to sit back and let your mind and heart mull over the recent past and upcoming future. You may feel inclined to do something which will benefit your health as you may have neglected it recently. Introspection comes naturally today.

Saturday 22nd

Today you can look at your inner compass from an objective viewpoint. You know that it is always there and are learning that some days you have more energy to work on it than others. This is an assessment day; make checks and gather resources for the road ahead.

Sunday 23rd

Your ruler turns direct today. Saturn has been in your sign for a long time and you may feel exhausted now. Spend time on self-love and treat yourself to something you desire. You may have intense feelings, but you need to slow down and breathe deeply.

Monday 24th

Your head and heart are having a little talk today. Just make sure that what you are hearing is not your inner critic. Listen to your heart and ignore words of self-doubt or negativity. Find a balance between personal time and couple time and you will achieve more successful outcomes.

Tuesday 25th

A new moon and solar eclipse may bring up intense emotions in the workplace. You may see issues of jealousy or control. Females will be highlighted. You may use these themes to make goals and intentions for career advancement, but avoid any drama or power struggles over the next two weeks.

Wednesday 26th

Hold on tight as this may be a day of volatile eruptions all over your workplace and family. An old issue from the past may re-surface and you may have difficulty dealing with it in a helpful way. This is not a reflection on you personally so stay strong.

Thursday 27th

You are in the mood for talking and intellectual discussion today. This will go down well in your social groups and you may find an outlet for your unexpressed worries. Online groups may be a place where you can share what you have learned about your personal growth this year.

Friday 28th

You may be tempted to make an impulse buy which is expensive and frivolous. You may have to chain your hands together and not let your wallet out of your pockets. It's possible that a spiritual group you were once interested in comes back into your awareness and you reconnect there.

Saturday 29th

Your energy may be very low. It's possible that you are drained or feel heavy and need to rest. This is essential to your mental health as you are about to enter a few days of introspection and need that time alone. Wind down and switch off from the world.

Sunday 30th

Mars turns retrograde today. You may notice that progress slows down which can be frustrating for a go-getter like you. Don't push romance now as it will push back. Looking after number one today may show you some unique new routines of self-care which will work for you.

Monday 31st

Hard work on your psyche no longer frightens you. You find another trigger and deal with it superbly. Not a lot is bothering you today and you are on top of your game. If your mood and mind seem at odds later, flow with them and see where they lead.

NOVEMBER
· · · · · · · · · · · · · · · · · · ·

Tuesday 1st

Everything seems like an uphill struggle today. The trick is not to take it personally. You may find that your duties are divided between home and work and you have difficulty making time for both. This will almost certainly tire you so make time at the end of the day for you.

Wednesday 2nd

What skills and talent can you revive today to help you with tasks? This may be anything which can restore balance and harmony in the workplace to money-making schemes. Your love life may be dragging you down and you are impatient to move forward. Accept that you can't right now.

Thursday 3rd

Today is much easier as you go with the flow more. Better communication is your most valuable asset now. You may notice that you are prioritising happiness over productivity, and this will be fine if it helps you to maintain a good balance of work and play.

Friday 4th

You manage to re-attach to your inner compass and have an emotional pull towards doing the things that you love. You may have to wait a while or accept that there are still small changes to be made before you can take that leap of faith and progress on your path.

Saturday 5th

Look out for irritations between home and work. You may be focusing on one side too much and neglecting the other. This will show up today and may cause you to re-think some strategies. It's impossible to please everyone but you do your best. Think about how you have managed this before.

Sunday 6th

Ensure that your conversations are clear today. You may come across as assertive or bossy in your love relationship. If you must play by the rules, then so do other people. It will ultimately benefit all to do so. Your mind may wander back into old hurts later.

Monday 7th

Today you may find that your need to love everyone equally is not accepted by some. You may see issues of jealousy or possessiveness arise. Don't seduce or be enticed into something which may be underhand and sneaky. It won't make you feel good in the long run.

Tuesday 8th

A full moon and lunar eclipse may show up how you have worked with your family or with things that you value. This could startle you into realising that some things are not worthy of your attention. Listen carefully for messages coming from your unconscious and take them seriously.

Wednesday 9th

Watch what you say today. There's a chance that gossip or rows can erupt and reveal deep secrets. This may begin a new process of letting something go as it no longer serves your best interests. Be discerning now and be kind if this includes people around you.

Thursday 10th

There is a double edged feel to today. You may be dreaming or searching the depths of your psyche. As a result, you may find golden nuggets of wisdom that will be useful now. At the same time, you feel restricted in your enquiries as not everyone is willing to discuss certain issues.

Friday 11th

Be mindful of your energy levels today. You may desire to be romantic or creative, but you simply don't have any enthusiasm. This will pass but, in the meantime, allow yourself this precious downtime to check in with your health. If something is too big, leave it for another time.

Saturday 12th

You may wish to feel nurtured and protected today. This is a good weekend for feeding your soul or getting all your mundane jobs done. You may have a chance to talk with someone special about deep and mysterious issues which are fascinating you at the moment. Be imaginative and intuitive.

Sunday 13th

Continue doing things you love today. Good food and company can assist in elevating your mood and bringing pleasant surprises. Emotionally, you will be on cloud nine enjoying sharing secrets and desires with someone you admire. Just make sure to keep one foot on the ground, ready for the coming week.

Monday 14th

Your intuition is high today and you may expect to understand a lot more than you realise. However, your sense of justice is also keen, and you may have to deal with something unpleasant. Partner time is essential this afternoon as you need to sound off to someone you trust.

Tuesday 15th

It's possible that a jealousy or control issue arises in the workplace. This may involve women and can be a discrimination or control issue. If you feel inclined to take this on yourself, you may make a formidable champion. It will rock some boats, but this may be needed.

Wednesday 16th

You may enter a time where your social life picks up pace. Make sure that you allow time for a partner too if they are not included in your wider groups. Communication needs to have absolute clarity today as there's a chance that you are tricked or deluded at work.

Thursday 17th

Reach out to your circle of friends as this may help you to discuss difficult topics in a safe place. This may also involve social media interest groups. You may find that something has grabbed your attention and you wish to explore more. Going deep may be scary but will bring you new understanding.

Friday 18th

You may be extra tired today so check what is more important and what you can do another time. Concentrate on making time for yourself as others may need you to help with something you just don't have the energy for. Avoid being dragged into other's business.

Saturday 19th

Your energy may be so low that a day in bed with a good book is all you can do. You may find it hard to concentrate and prefer to watch TV instead. Your mind is full of nonsense and you need to separate fact from fiction. If friends call, join them.

Sunday 20th

Your energy returns as does your sense of duty and responsibility. You may now see the need to get out and do simple chores that will get you through the day. Working through a checklist will be satisfying. Balancing everyone's requirements is a lot easier than you first thought.

Monday 21st

The workplace is highlighted, and you may see people coming and going. Is there anything you have forgotten to do? There may be a deadline and extra effort is needed. Your social groups are getting chatty and you could be in demand more in the coming weeks.

Tuesday 22nd

The Sun moves into your friends zone to enhance the new activity there. The Moon, however, is making you look at past problems you have faced within your family group and work arena. These may have surfaced again, and you try to recall how you settled them previously. Little surprises may unsettle you.

Wednesday 23rd

Don't let your emotions guide you today. They are more inclined to drift into fantasy thinking and will be biased. You must get a grip on reality and check all the facts. From there, you can make an informed decision if one is needed. Friends may give you impartial advice.

Thursday 24th

A new moon in your friends zone is another chance to start
something new and exciting with your social groups. You may
desire to spread your wings a little and visit overseas friends or
explore other cultures now. Jupiter turns direct and gives you
a big green go-ahead sign.

Friday 25th

Any recent excitement may have exhausted you and you
should pull back a little today. You need time to process new
thoughts and plans. Try not to make any commitments and
politely excuse yourself from groups until you have had time
to yourself. They will be waiting when you are ready.

Saturday 26th

Today has gentle energy which will enable you to take stock
of all that has happened recently. If you can switch off your
natural bias and judgement, sit as an observer, you may be able
to align yourself with new thoughts and perspectives. Make a
plan for steps to take.

Sunday 27th

Some things become clear to you today. You may have had to
swim through muddy waters to get there but you have. What
do you need to lovingly release from your life so that you have
room for something new? How can you do this in a fair manner?

Monday 28th

You wake feeling optimistic but tired. All this soul-searching
and recycling of old patterns can be exhausting. However, if
you refrain from making any major decisions just yet, you may
sail through the day gently. If you feel stuck, stay there and
look all around at what is challenging you.

Tuesday 29th

It may be that you are the centre of attention today which you enjoy. However, don't let this go to your head and stay humble. Conversations this evening may be tiresome or misunderstood. If someone is not hearing you, leave it and try again another day. Don't push it.

Wednesday 30th

You may have to lay the law down today if someone is being deliberately awkward. You can do this with compassion, so it won't be too bad. This may allow you to see that however much you value someone's presence; you are not their scapegoat. They must own responsibility too.

DECEMBER

. . . .

Thursday 1st

This is a very challenging day where stubbornness comes at you from all angles. You may have to divide your time between social groups and lovers. If you feel stuck in the middle, take a time-out and latch on to your inner compass. It's still there for whenever you need it.

Friday 2nd

Your dreams may be more vivid now and display the turbulence you are currently experiencing. Emotions when awake may be larger than usual as you try to connect to something surreal, possibly spiritual. Friends may inspire or ground you today. Be prepared to communicate your feelings to those close to you.

Saturday 3rd

A better day comes with easy interactions with your love life and social friendships. You may enjoy time with both or combine them. Maybe you take your lover to a party. Saturn, your ruler, is pleased with you for thinking of a solution to what may have been problematic.

Sunday 4th

Neptune turns direct today and your true north calls you once more. Your heart has a message for you, and you must listen carefully. This may involve a tweak of your plans, but this will benefit you in many ways. Be open to suggestions and advice now.

Monday 5th

Look to an elder or teacher who may offer you a lesson to put you back on track with self-development and following your dreams. You may have a sudden realisation of what it was you were meant to be doing all along. Unexpected help may come from family members today.

Tuesday 6th

Make sure that any plans and arrangements you have with friends are watertight as they may go astray over the coming festive season. You may need to make last-minute plans or cancellations. Big gestures are possible as you entertain the idea of spending time with a lover or creative project later today.

Wednesday 7th

This is a simple day where you just have to get enough done to get by. There are no major issues to deal with, but you may find that your mind turns inward and you are processing a lot of information. Hidden things will surface to be healed now.

Thursday 8th

A full moon in your romance zone shows you how much you have worked on love and creativity this year. Self-expression is also a theme and you may say something you have been longing to voice now. This may fill you with anticipation, but you are relieved when it is out there.

Friday 9th

You may be left feeling vulnerable and exposed today. Find your comfort zone and operate from inside its safety. You are not under attack, but you will function better if you believe you are safe. However, your heart may still give the game away as you speak your truth.

Saturday 10th

Today begins a few weeks of total self-love and care. It's possible that a lot of material comes up from your psyche now because you are in the right frame of mind to deal with it and heal it. You have all the resources you need to transform old wounds into a new you.

Sunday 11th

Let go of something you are fighting to control. You may not be meant to be in charge here. It's likely that you are clinging on to something that is no longer a fit. Let it go with love and grieve if you need to.

Monday 12th

You may feel uncomfortable and not know which way to turn. Look to your partner for comfort and support. Validation too if you feel the need for it. You wish to be outgoing and optimistic, but this needs a little extra effort. Success will come when you stay responsible and dutiful.

Tuesday 13th

Family members may be causing a disturbance which may make you want to rebel. Don't do it as this will drain your energy and make your boundaries weak. Stand up for your rights and be an example to others. Don't take on unnecessary baggage as it will weigh you down.

Wednesday 14th

Practice self-care today and have time alone if you need it.
Something as simple as cooking a favourite meal and a pamper
before bedtime will soothe those midweek blues. Grounding
activities can also help you to come back to your centre of
calm and positivity. Give it a try.

Thursday 15th

There is a huge amount of earthy energy today which you
may not like. However, right now you may be flying too far
away and need to come back to base. You may be surprised
at how much this helps and can talk to others about your
inner work.

Friday 16th

If you need to make yourself small and invisible today, you
can do this by managing your everyday duties and leaving
dreaming for another time. You may feel more productive if
you knuckle down to the daily grind and declutter ready for
the festive season. It will also make you feel fresh.

Saturday 17th

You may not be in the mood for either love or family matters
today. Creative and romantic pursuits may weigh heavy on you
as will introspection. The best thing you can do now is to let
your mind explore the possibility of bringing more harmony
into your life.

· · · · · · · · · · · · · · · · · ·

Sunday 18th

A day of duty and responsibility awaits you. There are some things you just can't change so don't waste your energy trying. Reach out to other lands or cultures to satisfy an itch you may have regarding higher education, religion or philosophies.

Monday 19th

Today you have an intense frame of mind which will help to get your work done. You may have a razor-sharp perception of the more difficult challenges in the workplace, but you get to the bottom of them easily. Let no-one distract you from this as you will gain points from the boss and be seen in a favourable light.

Tuesday 20th

You have many big ideas today, but don't be in a rush to implement them, they can wait. Family obligations arise and cause tension. These can be appeased by letting others know that you have stuff to do and will return later to see to their needs.

Wednesday 21st

The winter solstice arrives with the shortest day and this may make you hurry through your chores. A midweek social event may be nice as will a time to rest. Pause, reflect and contemplate on the year gone by, and congratulate yourself on how much you have grown and developed your inner world.

Thursday 22nd

There is no time for dreaming as you may have deadlines to meet before the holidays. You are more than ready for a break, but you are also conscious of what needs to be done first. Put family and romantic matters on hold until you have done your work.

Friday 23rd

There is a new moon today which can help you set goals and intentions regarding your private, inner life. Self-development is an ongoing process and when you see how far you have come this year you will be willing to dig even deeper to become the best version of you yet.

Saturday 24th

It will be difficult to find time for you today but when you do, it will be worth it. Your heart and mind are in sync and allow you to feel good about yourself. A great sense of where you are and where you are heading lets you dream a little today.

Sunday 25th

Enjoy the festive fun. Your self-control will help you to contribute to the celebrations and do your bit without complaint. There is plenty of love to go around and you may be the one who is giving it. Keep a little back for yourself.

Monday 26th

Watch your energy levels today as your family may be demanding too much from you. This may result in a mini tantrum just to blow off steam. Stay out of aggravations that don't involve you and make sure that personal boundaries are strong and protected. Be mature and responsible at this time.

Tuesday 27th

This is a dreamy day when you can kick back and relax.
You may wish to do this alone or with someone very special.
It might be a time where you choose to do some introspection
that has a more spiritual element. Place real value on the
connections you make.

Wednesday 28th

Your inner compass and true north are waiting for you today.
You may find that you have already made plans for next year
which will help you to follow your dreams and visions. If the
festive season is tiring you, withdraw and practise self-care
today as it will balance you.

Thursday 29th

Just as the year is almost finished, Mercury turns retrograde.
This may not be so bad as it will involve your private life.
You may feel that this gives you a chance to re-visit what has
surfaced for you and to assess their new meanings in your life.

Friday 30th

Although your energy is telling you to run, you may just have
to walk today as your goals are not visible and you will have
to wait. Slow down the pace and enjoy the remainder of the
holidays. Romance can be satisfying but not as exciting as you
would like.

Saturday 31st

Don't let anyone tell you how to enjoy the last day of 2022. You may have a testing time or be in demand from different quarters. If you desire to stay in and have an early night, then do it. Take care of yourself and see to your own needs.

Aquarius

....

PEOPLE WHO SHARE
YOUR SIGN

PEOPLE WHO SHARE YOUR SIGN

· · · · · · · · · · · · · · · · · ·

Born to be different and shake things up, Aquarians are the liberating air sign that are prepared to ruffle some feathers if needed. From the speeches of Abraham Lincoln to the words of Virginia Woolf, the unique insight and intellect that so many Aquarians have make them a sign to be listened to and take notice of. Discover which of these individualist Aquarians share your exact birthday with and see if you can spot the similarities.

21st January
BooBoo Stewart (1994), Jerry Trainor (1977), Emma Bunton (1976), Geena Davis (1956), Paul Allen (1953), Billy Ocean (1950), Plácido Domingo (1941), Benny Hill (1924), Christian Dior (1905), Grigori Rasputin (1869)

22nd January
Silentó (1998), Logic (1990), Hidetoshi Nakata (1977), Gabriel Macht (1972), Guy Fieri (1968), Diane Lane (1965), Linda Blair (1959), Steve Perry (1949), John Hurt (1940)

23rd January
Doutzen Kroes (1985), Draya Michele (1985), Arjen Robben (1984), Tito Ortiz (1975), Tiffani Thiessen (1974), Mariska Hargitay (1964), Princess Caroline of Hanover (1957), Richard Dean Anderson (1950), Édouard Manet (1832)

24th January

Luis Suárez (1987), Mischa Barton (1986), Justin Baldoni (1984), Frankie Grande (1983), Tatyana Ali (1979), Kristen Schaal (1978), Ed Helms (1974), Kenya Moore (1971), Sharon Tate (1943)

25th January

Calum Hood (1996), Robinho (1984), Alicia Keys (1981), Xavi (1980), Princess Charlene of Monaco (1978), Virginia Woolf (1882)

26th January

Colin O'Donoghue (1981), Brendan Rodgers (1973), José Mourinho (1963), Wayne Gretzky (1961), Ellen DeGeneres (1958), Eddie Van Halen (1955), Angela Davis (1944), Paul Newman (1925), Louis Zamperini (1917), Maria von Trapp (1905)

27th January

Rosamund Pike (1979), Patton Oswalt (1969), Alan Cumming (1965), Bridget Fonda (1964), Narciso Rodriguez (1961), Mimi Rogers (1956), Mikhail Baryshnikov (1948), Beatrice Tinsley (1941), Lewis Carroll (1832)

28th January

Ariel Winter (1998), Will Poulter (1993), J. Cole (1985), Elijah Wood (1981), Nick Carter (1980), Gianluigi Buffon (1978), Rick Ross (1976), Carlos Slim (1940), Alan Alda (1936)

29th January

Adam Lambert (1982), Sara Gilbert (1975), Heather Graham (1970), Oprah Winfrey (1954), Tom Selleck (1945), Katharine Ross (1940), Anton Chekhov (1860)

30th January

Eiza González (1990), Arda Turan (1987), Wilmer Valderrama (1980), Christian Bale (1974), Phil Collins (1951), Dick Cheney, U.S. Vice President (1941), Franklin D. Roosevelt, U.S. President (1882)

31st January

Amy Jackson (1992), Marcus Mumford (1987), Justin Timberlake (1981), Kerry Washington (1977), Portia de Rossi (1973), Minnie Driver (1970), Daniel Moder (1969), John Lydon (1956), Jonathan Banks (1947), Carol Channing (1921), Jackie Robinson (1919), Baba Vanga (1911)

1st February

Harry Styles (1994), Heather Morris (1987), Ronda Rousey (1987), Lauren Conrad (1986), Abbi Jacobson (1984), Michael C. Hall (1971), Lisa Marie Presley (1968), Princess Stéphanie of Monaco (1965), Langston Hughes (1902), Clark Gable (1901)

2nd February

Gerard Piqué (1987), Gemma Arterton (1986), Gemma Collins (1981), Christine Bleakley (1979), Shakira (1977), Christie Brinkley (1954), Duncan Bannatyne (1949), Farrah Fawcett (1947), David Jason (1940), Ayn Rand (1905), James Joyce (1882)

3rd February

Sean Kingston (1990), Elizabeth Holmes (1984), Amal Clooney (1978), Isla Fisher (1976), Warwick Davis (1970), Maura Tierney (1965), Joachim Löw (1960), Nathan Lane (1956), Blythe Danner (1943), Norman Rockwell (1894)

4th February

Hannibal Buress (1983), Gavin DeGraw (1977), Cam'ron (1976), Natalie Imbruglia (1975), Oscar De La Hoya (1973), Alice Cooper (1948), Rosa Parks (1913), Charles Lindbergh (1902)

5th February

Neymar (1992), Darren Criss (1987), Kevin Gates (1986), Cristiano Ronaldo (1985), Carlos Tevez (1984), Tiwa Savage (1980), Tim Meadows (1961), Michael Sheen (1969), Laura Linney (1964), Duff McKagan (1964), Jennifer Jason Leigh (1962)

6th February

Tinashe (1993), Dane DeHaan (1986), Alice Eve (1982), Rick Astley (1966), Axl Rose (1962), Kathy Najimy (1957), Bob Marley (1945), Ronald Reagan, U.S. President (1911), Babe Ruth (1895)

7th February

Bea Miller (1999), Jacksepticeye (1990), Deborah Ann Woll (1985), Ashton Kutcher (1978), Chris Rock (1965), Garth Brooks (1962), Eddie Izzard (1962), James Spader (1960), Laura Ingalls Wilder (1876), Charles Dickens (1812)

8th February

Klay Thompson (1990), Seth Green (1974), Mauricio Macri, Argentinian President (1959), Mary Steenburgen (1953), John Williams (1932), James Dean (1931), Dmitri Mendeleev (1834), Jules Verne (1828)

9th February

Michael B. Jordan (1987), Rose Leslie (1987), Tom Hiddleston (1981), Zhang Ziyi (1979), Charlie Day (1976), Amber Valletta (1974), Chris Gardner (1954), Mia Farrow (1945), Alice Walker (1944), Joe Pesci (1943), Carole King (1942)

10th February

Chloë Grace Moretz (1997), Emma Roberts (1991), Radamel Falcao (1986), Uzo Aduba (1981), Stephanie Beatriz (1981), Holly Willoughby (1981), Don Omar (1978), Elizabeth Banks (1974), Laura Dern (1967), Bertolt Brecht (1898)

11th February

Taylor Lautner (1992), Natalie Dormer (1982), Kelly Rowland (1981), Damian Lewis (1971), Jennifer Aniston (1969), Sarah Palin (1964), Sheryl Crow (1962), Burt Reynolds (1936), Leslie Nielsen (1926), Thomas Edison (1847)

12th February

Mike Posner (1988), Iko Uwais (1983), Gucci Mane (1980), Christina Ricci (1980), Naseem Hamed (1974), Josh Brolin (1968), Chris McCandless (1968), Charles Darwin (1809), Abraham Lincoln, U.S. President (1809)

13th February

Memphis Depay (1994), Mena Suvari (1979), Robbie Williams (1974), Kelly Hu (1968), Peter Gabriel (1950), Jerry Springer (1944), Kim Novak (1933)

14th February

Freddie Highmore (1992), Ángel Di María (1988), Edinson Cavani (1987), Danai Gurira (1978), Jim Jefferies (1977), Rob Thomas (1972), Simon Pegg (1970), Michael Bloomberg (1942)

15th February

Gary Clark Jr. (1984), Alex Borstein (1971), Shepard Fairey (1970), Chris Farley (1964), Matt Groening (1954), Janice Dickinson (1955), Jane Seymour (1951), Irena Sendler (1874), Susan B. Anthony (1820)

16th February

The Weeknd (1990), Elizabeth Olsen (1989), Valentino Rossi (1979), Philipp Plein (1978), Amanda Holden (1971), Christopher Eccleston (1964), John McEnroe (1959), Ice-T (1958), Eckhart Tolle (1948)

17th February

Marc Márquez (1993), Ed Sheeran (1991), Bonnie Wright (1991), Joseph Gordon-Levitt (1981), Paris Hilton (1981), Billie Joe Armstrong (1972), Denise Richards (1971), Michael Jordan (1963), Rene Russo (1954)

18th February

Le'Veon Bell (1992), Jeremy Allen White (1991), Jillian Michaels (1974), Molly Ringwald (1968), Dr. Dre (1965), Matt Dillon (1964), John Travolta (1954), Cybill Shepherd (1950), Paco Rabanne (1934), Yoko Ono (1933), Toni Morrison (1931), Enzo Ferrari (1898)

19th February

Mauro Icardi (1993), Victoria Justice (1993), Arielle Kebbel (1985), David Gandy (1980), Seal (1963), Benicio del Toro (1957), Jeff Daniels (1955), Tony Iommi (1948), Cristina Fernández de Kirchner, Argentinian President (1953)